YOU ARE
NOT ALONE

YOU ARE NOT ALONE

＊

*Words of
Experience and Hope
for the Journey
Through Depression*

＊

JULIA THORNE

with LARRY ROTHSTEIN

HarperPerennial
A Division of HarperCollins*Publishers*

For Tom

Copyright acknowledgments follow page 185.

YOU ARE NOT ALONE. Copyright © 1993 by Julia Thorne. All rights reserved.
Printed in the United States of America. No part of this book may be used
or reproduced in any manner whatsoever without written permission except
in the case of brief quotations embodied in critical articles and reviews. For
information address HarperCollins Publishers, Inc., 10 East 53rd Street, New
York, NY 10022.

HarperCollins books may be purchased for educational, business, or sales
promotional use. For information, please write: Special Markets Department,
HarperCollins Publishers, Inc., 10 East 53rd Street, New York, NY 10022.

FIRST EDITION

Designed by Jessica Shatan

Library of Congress Cataloging-in-Publication Data
Thorne, Julia, 1944–
    You are not alone : words of experience and hope for the journey
through depression / by Julia Thorne with Larry Rothstein. — 1st ed.
        p. cm.
    ISBN 0-06-096977-6 (pbk.)
    1. Depression, Mental—Popular works. I. Rothstein, Larry. II. Title.
RC537.T5   1993
616.85'27—dc20   92-56255

93 94 95 96 97 ❖/RRD 10 9 8 7 6 5 4 3 2 1

CONTENTS

INTRODUCTION

*F*ebruary 1980, five months after my 36th birthday, my mind ravaged by corroding voices, my body defeated by bone-rattling panics, I sat on the edge of my bed minutes from taking my life. For weeks I had silently prepared my death. I believed I was a failure. I could no longer pretend I was of use to my husband or my children. I was too tired. I needed to lie down, curled up, never to wake again. I knew that, once I was gone, my family and friends would be relieved of the burden of my incompetency.

I was emotionally, spiritually, and physically exhausted by a life-destroying affliction—depression. . . . I was also alone—dying a lonely death in a vacuum of misunderstanding, ignorance, and shame.

To the uninformed observer I had no external reason to be depressed. I had everything supposedly essential for happiness and well-being. I had two beautiful, healthy, intelligent daughters; a handsome, successful husband; a sprawling house in an affluent suburb. I had had a privileged international upbringing with homes in America and Europe. A fairy tale come true? Hardly. Behind the enviable externals was a nightmare life defined by self-hate and self-doubt, a life sapped by the pain of depression from which, I had come to believe, death was the only escape.

I Was Not Alone

Although I did not know it in 1980, I was not alone. An estimated 21 million Americans experience some form of depression each year. Women, especially young mothers, suffer twice as frequently as men. One out of two Americans have family members afflicted by depression. Americans today are ten times more depressed than their grandparents were. Most sobering, of the millions of depressed Americans, many will commit suicide if not treated appropriately. Suicide is now the second leading killer of children and adolescents.

I knew none of this in 1980. I found it out as I got well. Getting well was a process of educating myself about depression and discovering truths that allowed me to accept the despair I was periodically paralyzed by.

One of the ways I educated myself was to observe how people around me hid their depressions, afraid to speak out or get help, terrified of the stigma attached to emotional illness. I listened to their stories, denials, and loneliness and witnessed the self-destructive habits they had developed to distract themselves from their pain.

I began to talk with people who I knew suffered from depression. They appeared to have had common experiences somewhere in their lives, particularly as children: emotional deprivation, trauma, loss, abuse, addiction, abandonment, or other circumstances that damaged self-esteem and a sense of potential self. Depression clearly resulted from individual experiences and conditions.

Searching out professional support for two depressed members of my family, I soon learned that depression is frequently a family condition whose biology and behaviors are passed down as reliably as hair color. With the help of a therapist, I drew a family tree marking each relevant antecedent or contemporary with red ink. Without much effort, I had sketched boughs laden with the crimson fruits of my inheritance. I could trace depression and depressive behavior back to my great-grandparents.

I discovered—not surprisingly—that depression attracts depression. I and other members of my family had married individuals with histories of depression in their families, too. I might be the first person to admit it, but I was not the only one to suffer from it.

Redefining Depression

As I continued my healing, I learned depression was once the traditional path to "soul fitness," the way exercise is the path to body fitness today. For hundreds of years, melancholy was treasured as the characteristic of creative genius, the introspective quality that gave birth to great talent, leadership, and invention. I began to ask myself: If depression was once of use, could it not be converted into alliance again?

Was emotional pain a psychic signal the way physical pain warned of something amiss in my body? If it was, then I could listen to it. Perhaps I could stop using combative and domineering language—"beating depression," "overcoming depression." Maybe I was wasting my energy trying to eradicate depression; maybe I could refocus that energy on understanding what it had to teach me.

A memory nagged at me as well as the questions. It was a

memory of passion: a full and committed participation in the experience of life, with all its melancholy and joy, pain and pleasure, fear and courage, anger and humor, grief and love. Passion had been the common denominator of my social experience as I grew up in Italy from the age of 8 to 24. I had happy and vital memories of how that social experience had helped me survive.

In Italy I had known happiness. Couldn't I know it again? I said to myself in Italian: I need to regain my *anima* and *spirito*. *Anima* is the Italian word for "soul," but it can also mean "feeling." (The verb *animare* means "to give life to" or "to enliven"; someone *animato* is lively.) The Italian *spirito* also has more than one meaning: "spirit" and "wit." (Someone *spiritoso* is not only witty but also amusing, fun to be with.) My memories of Italy—of well-being and freedom in a full emotional life—gave me the hope that I could want to live again.

If I needed to regain my spirit and find my soul, and if spirit and soul required a passionate or full emotional experience, then melancholy, pain, fear, anger, and grief were essential ingredients. Clearly, emotions were energy—fundamental resources of psychic nutrition. I should not be avoiding depression, I should be tending its garden, nourishing my spirit with the produce of its reality.

The Journey Through Depression

I drew hope from history and my memories of Italy. Others had survived the turmoils of depression. I had once known a way to live with darkness. Lashing myself to the raft of that hope, I set out on an emotional, physical, intellectual, and spiritual journey in search of healing.

Step-by-step, one question, one memory, one feeling, and one experience at a time, I made depression my ally. I let it highlight a slow rediscovery of myself, a line-by-line reprogramming of my habits and thought processes.

Today I describe myself as "free" of depression. The monsters of despair have been transformed into loyal companions, emotional guard dogs who protect me and warn of trouble. The slimy murk has dried up. The darkness has become a beacon for healing, peace of mind, and a sense of freedom.

All of this does not mean I am not visited by depression; I am. But depression no longer chains me, nor weighs me down, nor imprisons me. It has become a mentor and guide. Today I am free to be creative with the experience of depression, to work with its pain for an ever more fulfilling and passionate life.

It Takes Time

It took time to be free. It was a slow, frightening process that required descending repeatedly to the bottom of the emotional well where I had banished and "de-pressed" my unwanted emotions. I needed to retrieve the potential self I was born with. To retrieve that self I had to become intimate with who I wanted to be, which meant being intimate with my emotions, all my emotions, especially the abandoned ones like sadness and anger.

Twice at the bottom of the emotional well I lost the strength to climb back out. I wanted to give up and put an end to my pain. To survive those crises I used antidepressant medication for short periods of time. I could not have done the therapeutic work of understanding my pain without the support and relief it provided.

Healing the spirit requires surrendering to pain in much the same way the body, at the request of the immune system, surrenders to fever when wounded by infection. Medication and other therapeutic techniques can and should be used to ease the discomfort, but healing requires identifying both the properties of infection and the time to recover.

Surrendering to pain is frightening. There are no short cuts—no quick fixes. Living as we do today in a culture addicted to sensationalism, external gratification, and escapism, many of us feel spiritually weak, terrified of the dark side of life. Imprisoned by that terror, we feel adrift, without spiritual comfort, and unable to live full and passionate lives that include all our emotions and potential.

The Need for Support

Surrendering to pain requires courage. Some of the courage I needed was mine, but a great deal was on loan. I have never, nor will I ever, consciously explore the depths of depression without unconditional support. Even 13 years ago, when, alone and undiagnosed, I wanted to take my life, a little internal voice guided me to help. Today, when I arrive at dark and frightening stages in my journey, I have a gang—special friends, my women's support group, my therapist, a Zen master—with safety nets, ropes, flashlights, food and water, and encouraging words to accompany me to safety.

Why I Wrote This Book

I am not alone. Not in the greater world, not in the smaller world of my family, not in history, not in myself. And you are not alone. For that reason, I created The Depression Initiative, a nonprofit educational foundation that focuses on bringing support and information on depression to the general public through a series of media products.

This book has been created as part of that effort. *You Are Not Alone* intends to reach out and embrace you with the hope, understanding, acceptance, empathy, and support you may not have—to offer permission and acceptance and a path to help.

With appropriate diagnosis and treatment, more than 80 percent of those afflicted can have their symptoms alleviated. The sad truth is that only a fraction of those who need help seek it.

In my case, seeking any kind of literature that would comfort me and offer simple guidance, all I could find in bookstores and libraries were technical tomes or self-help manuals. By page 10 of these books I was overwhelmed, unable to concentrate, and, in my perceived failure to meet the standards of the book, further convinced I was incompetent.

Where was the literature that spoke of what other people do? Was there a book designed for the short attention span of the depression sufferer? What book belonged to the sufferer? What book enabled sufferers to feel unthreatened and safe, to make their friend independent of any outside instructions or control? Where was the book in *their* voices rather than in a third person's? Where were the first-person tales of hope and survival?

Unable to find what I needed, I conceived a book on depression that had never been written before: a book for individuals, in the voice of individuals. I traveled around the country interviewing everyone who was willing to identify themselves as either suffering from depression, in a relationship with someone with a depressive experience, or treating individuals and families suffering from depression.

Men and women of all ages, socioeconomic environments, cultures, and ethnicities told me their stories. From these stories I structured first-person composites, changing names and locations in order to protect individual privacy.

How to Use This Book

What this cooperative effort nurtured is a book unique in size, style, construction, and content, designed to keep you company and act as a nonjudgmental and supportive friend you hear from and talk to, a friend who has tools to survive just as you have. Interlaced with the first-person accounts are pages printed in italics in which I share some of the tools of my recovery. These pages have blank spaces in which you may wish to write or draw feelings, thoughts, or information.

The first section, "You Are Not Alone," affirms the communality of the feelings of depression in a variety of situations. "Words of Hope," the next section, is drawn from people who have begun to search for support and healing. The coping tools, strategies, and activities of individuals who have recovered from depression or are working toward emotional well-being are reflected in the third section, "The Experience of Healing." A fourth section, "Concerned Voices," echoes the feelings of those who love us, work with us, and are associated with us. The last section, "Seeking Help," lists individual and institutional resources available for help. Finally, there is a guide to the signs of depression.

This Is Your Book

There are no rules attached to this book. You can ignore the blanks if you wish. You can draw a line through anything you don't like—paste something over it, color it out, write over it. Open the book at any page or start at the beginning. Start at the end. There is no "correct" way to read it. This book is yours to use any way you want.

But please take your time. Despite its apparent simplicity, this is a powerful book full of intense emotion. Some of our advisers have suggested reading it bit by bit, perhaps no more than three pages at a time. If any of the stories bring up feelings you find hard to bear, stop reading. At that time it might be helpful to take several deep breaths. You might put on some music, or find someone to talk to, or take a hot bath, or do some other activity you like. And, if it helps, when you are ready write down your feelings.

Daily Strength for Daily Needs

When I was a little girl my godmother gave me a book given to her by her grandmother. Published in 1910, it is titled *Daily Strength for Daily Needs*. A small volume bound in garnet leather with gold embossing, its Preface describes it as "intended for a daily companion and counsellor . . . to strengthen the reader . . . to bear the burdens of each day with . . . courage." Each page, representing a day of the year, includes verse, prose, and excerpts from the Bible. It was my godmother's family tradition to write in important events or thoughts on relevant days and to add to the book's wisdom personal letters, newspaper clippings, verses, and so on to remember or refer to. The book was to be kept near one at all times and reused like a poem, song, or memory that gives inspiration and hope. Over the years, I have written in it and folded letters and other printed matter between its pages, letting my own milestones, feelings, and thoughts have root next to those of my godmother until, bulging with our lives, the book is now tied closed with a white shoelace.

You Are Not Alone has the same intent: to be used over and over, to be filled with your own notes and mementos, to be revisited like a trusted friend who reminds you of who you are, where you have been, what you can do, where you can go. It embraces a community of age and experience. As the voices in this book testify, you are not alone, you never were alone, and you never need feel alone again.

PART I

YOU ARE NOT ALONE

✳

There Are
Many Voices
to the Experience
of Depression

✳

Where we had thought to be alone, we should be with all the world.

—JOSEPH CAMPBELL, THE HERO WITH A THOUSAND FACES

"Brainstorm," . . . *has unfortunately been preempted to describe, somewhat jocularly, intellectual inspiration . . . Told that someone's mood disorder has evolved into a storm—a veritable howling tempest in the brain, which is indeed what a clinical depression resembles like nothing else—even the uninformed layman might display sympathy rather than the standard reaction that "depression" evokes, something akin to "So what?" or "You'll pull out of it" or "We all have bad days."*

—WILLIAM STYRON, DARKNESS VISIBLE

IT'S SO LONELY BEING DEPRESSED

How can you tell anyone how you feel when you're depressed? No one wants to be around someone who's down. Who wants to spend time with someone who's full of fear, anger, and sadness? That's a real downer.

Besides, I don't know anyone who's gone through what I'm going through now. What can I say to a friend? That I want to check out, that I want to go to sleep and never wake up, that I'm so terrified of life that I can't get up in the morning, that I'm becoming a victim of delusions and hysteria? Nobody wants to hear that. People will think I'm some kind of nut case, that I'm a wimp, a weakling.

It's so lonely being depressed.

Clara
Santa Fe, New Mexico
age 50

FEAR

I fear everything and everyone. I fear being forgotten and overlooked.

Grant
Richmond, West Virginia
age 32

VOICES

I want the pain of the voices in my head to stop. There are all these voices telling me I'm a bad person. I feel like a helpless child being punished for all the things I've done wrong. I can't seem to call on any of the adult parts of me. I can't get away from the voices. Everyday it's the same. The voices are making me sick.

Katherine
Lincoln, Massachusetts
age 52

INADEQUACY

I feel like I'm nobody. I call the feeling "comparison distress."
I go to a party and I listen to all these women doing all these
fascinating things—lawyers, board members, TV production,
teaching. I'm just a mother and housewife. I hold back. I
don't talk. In my silence I feel even more inadequate than
before. I want to crumble in the corner of a room. Instead, I
stay standing, pretending I'm listening, while inside myself
I'm giving myself a lot of "self-talk." I say things like, "Louise,
stay right where you are. If you sit down it will be worse.
Louise, keep that smile on your face. Nod intelligently." I just
want to disappear, evaporate. I feel so empty, such a waste of
everyone's time.

Louise
Chicago, Illinois
age 44

Who Am I?

My family doesn't know who I am. When I was a teenager, I would say to my mother, "I feel depressed." She would scold me, "No you don't! You have nothing to feel depressed about!" But I did. I wasn't allowed to have any feelings. So when I was sad or angry or lonely I was told I wasn't. I began to think I was a bad girl to have those feelings. I learned to shut whole parts of me down.

I think depressed people have lost a sense of who they are.

Margaret
Akron, Ohio
age 27

REFLECTIONS

In 1980, when I was in therapy for the first time, my therapist would ask me, "What are you feeling?" I would always answer, "What do you mean?" He would gently encourage me to identify emotions and try to describe them. Slowly I learned to say, "I feel angry," "I feel scared," "I feel lonely." For the first time I was allowing myself to express my feelings. I began to value all of myself.

—Julia

FEAR OF FAILURE

Sometimes I just break into a sweat. I'll be sitting at my desk—the hotshot corporate lawyer—in New York City, thirty floors above Fifth Avenue. The sun is shining. I can see the sparkle on the lake in Central Park. In the next room is the best secretary in the whole world. I have a beautiful country house in Connecticut, the perfect blonde wife, more money than I know what to do with. Yet there I am sweating in a panic behind my desk. If I could open the window, I'd jump out.

How can I say I'm not happy? Look at everything I have. Who'd believe me? Who can I talk to? How do I know one friend wouldn't tell another friend, etc., etc., until it got back to the partners? It's a dog-eat-dog world out there. There are a lot of people who'd do anything for my job. Boy, would that be embarrassing!

Tell me who you know that would want their million-dollar legal work done by a person suffering from depression? The first thing a client would say is, "I don't want that guy touching my case!" The first thing the partners of my law firm would say is, "I don't think Sam is up to handling a challenging case." Then slowly they'd pull all my work away and I'd be a professional cripple with nothing to distract me from my emotional anguish. If they took my work away, who would I be?

Who would I be without all this? I don't know how to be anything else. What would people think of me if I wasn't rich and successful? So I sit at my desk on a beautiful clear day in a panic about losing it all, in a panic about failing, in a panic about making it through a day without wanting to jump out the window. You know what I think? I think, if I admitted I was depressed, if I failed and lost it all, I might not exist. That's a lot of pressure. It's scary. I'm trapped.

Sam
New York, New York
age 52

I'm No one

The second time I felt suicidal I went to a psychiatric hospital. A young psychiatrist came to talk to me. He sat on a chair at the end of my bed. He said, "I'm going to ask you a question. If you don't feel ready to answer it, that's OK." Then he asked, "Who's Allegra?"

I panicked. "What do you mean?" I asked back.

"When you look inside, who do you see?"

It was horrible. When I looked inside I couldn't see anyone. All I saw was a black hole. I had no idea who I was, if there was anyone. "Oh my God!" I thought, "I'm no one."

Allegra
Brookline, Massachusetts
age 48

WORTHLESS

Whenever I get depressed it's because I've lost a sense of self. I can't find reasons to like myself. I think I'm ugly. I think no one likes me. I can't make decisions. I take no pleasure in any of the things I usually like doing. I'm always bored. I don't bother to wash my hair. I start eating everything I can get my hands on. I gain a lot of weight. My clothes don't fit. I'll wear the same sweat shirt and pants for days. I don't call my friends. I become grumpy and short-tempered. Nobody wants to be around me. I'm left alone. Being alone confirms that I am ugly and not worth being with. I think I'm responsible for everything that goes wrong. I told my husband that the epitaph on my tombstone should read, "It was all her fault."

Greta
Provo, Utah
age 27

HOLIDAYS

I dread holidays. Especially Christmas and Easter because they're family holidays. There is so much expectation for happiness and love. All my memories are of exhaustion. I cooked for days, the kids fought, and my husband bickered about how much money we spent.

I hate holidays. And you know what? My friends without families feel the same way. They have fantasies of the happiness they see advertised that never existed for them.

The other thing that no one ever admits about holidays is that they are sad. They mark the passage of time and, in my case, because I'm older, of loss.

No wonder there's so much depression at holiday times.

Maggie

Peoria, Illinois

age 69

REFLECTIONS

Sometimes my feelings were overwhelming and I'd feel as if I couldn't bear them in my body. Then I'd remember a friend's words: "Take long, slow breaths, in and out, and let your feelings move through you. Then write them down, put them on a piece of paper outside your body."

—Julia

program

KNIFE-EDGE SHARP

Everything in my body is knife-edge sharp. Every breath has an edge, too. Every piece of food stings in my mouth. Either I have too much saliva or no saliva at all, so I choke or can't swallow. My eyes water or dry out. I can see things other people can't see—I can see colors in people's bodies. I can see inside mine. I can see in some way that I'm not thriving. That makes me panic. I'm afraid of not thriving, but I don't know what to do to thrive. How do you tell someone you're not thriving inside?

Anna
Jackson, Wyoming
age 40

I Didn't Want My Baby

I was 27. I had just given birth to my second child—she was two weeks old. A little girl. I'd wanted a little girl so desperately. I remember waking up one morning feeling hopeless. I was fine when I went to bed. I just woke up with this awful dread in my throat and chest—like a big lump. I was spiraling downward into a bottomless well, drowning. Suddenly, from one day to the next, I saw no future. I didn't want the baby anymore. Day after day it got worse. I couldn't sleep. The anxiety was constant. I was full of fear. I cried and cried. I had these voices—these voices running uncontrollably free in my head. I couldn't breathe. It was terrifying.

When I went to my ob/gyn for my six-week checkup, I tried to tell him. I said, "I can't cope. I don't want to wake up in the morning. I can't handle the feelings anymore." He couldn't hear me. He patted me on the back and told me it would pass. But I thought I was going crazy. I couldn't walk into my house. I didn't want to see my husband or my baby. Oh! It was horrible, really horrible.

Virginia
Eugene, Oregon
age 31

THE SOUND OF MY VOICE

Sometimes I can't talk. I hate the sound of my voice. I hate the sound of anyone else's voice. If people talk to me, I want to hit them.

So I get in my truck and head for the country. I drive as fast as I can. Sometimes I wonder what it would be like to steer right off the road at 100 miles an hour.

Other times I can't help talking. I see someone and I talk and talk and talk. I want to shut up but I can't. I hurt so bad. I get so tired of talking I got to go to a bar and get drunk. I can't stop talking 'til I pass out.

Willie Joe
Lubbock, Texas
age 21

EMOTIONAL STEAMROLLER

I know what I'm doing, believe it or not. I just don't know how to stop. I'm afraid if I stop, all my feelings will catch up with me and I'll be overwhelmed. I'm afraid all my sadness and anger will flatten me like a steamroller, so I just keep going.

I'm very successful. I own a huge commercial real estate company. I love the challenge. I work seven days a week. I've also got two adorable kids, but I don't see them much. I have to stop thinking about work to be with the kids and then the feelings start creeping in.

My ex-husband says he wouldn't have divorced me if I had come home more often. Who knows? You know, it takes two to tango! Anyway, I'm not lonely. I have lots of relationships, so I can call some guy up and have a good time. There's nothing like sex to dull the loneliness and keep depression at bay. I guess I miss being loved, but when I think about that I just find another project to start.

Margo
Miami, Florida
age 39

CAR CRASH

Both my sons were killed four years ago in a car crash. A truck jack-knifed on the highway and hit them. They were pinned inside the car. Before they could be rescued from the wreckage, the car caught fire and they were burned up.

It's hard to look into the future. It's too depressing without my sons. Things will happen at the office that remind me of the kids. One of their friends will call to say hi, or an employee will tell me his son is getting married. Then the grief becomes overwhelming. Tears come to my eyes.

But I can't show it. I can't be sad around my clients. I'm responsible for the management of large amounts of their money. People do not want to invest money with someone they think is depressed. I have to hide my feelings. I have to push my feelings down inside. Pushing the feelings away takes a lot of effort. Sometimes I feel so tired I have to take a nap. I'll tell my secretary not to disturb me, and I'll lie down on the sofa in my office. But I always feel guilty. I don't believe I should still feel this sad.

Larry
Portland, Oregon
age 64

REFLECTIONS

My father's death was crippling—literally. Within months of his death I couldn't walk without crutches. Several doctors found nothing wrong with me. I even had surgery. Slowly my therapist helped me see that my physical pain and handicap was the only language I had for the emotional pain of my father's loss. He suggested I write about my pain to identify it in words.

—Julia

MY PAIN REMINDS ME I'M ALIVE

When I'm depressed, pain is my best friend. I wallow in my
pain. It's what I am familiar with. I'll tell you that I hate my
pain and that there is nothing good about it, but I still hold
on to it. I'm so dead inside, so empty of any enthusiasm or
hope. My pain reminds me I'm alive. It allows me to be angry.
Anger is the only emotion I can feel. I can be angry at my
body, at my family, angry at having to work so hard, angry at
the pain I have to feel. It's the only emotion I can feel. I
think if I couldn't feel the anger, I wouldn't feel anything. I'd
wonder if I was alive. I'm scared of dying, so I need my pain
and anger.

George
Bellingham, Washington
age 30

Hitting My Children

I don't like myself after I've hit one of my kids. I don't mean to. It's that sometimes life gets overwhelming. Especially in the evening. My husband's been laid off. We haven't got enough money. The pressure to survive is almost more than I can bear. My husband goes to the bar sometimes before he comes home. So I'll come back from work at the grocery store and be alone with the kids, so tired I can hardly stand up. They're tired too. They've been in day care all day. I'll be making them supper when all I want to do is go to bed. I resent making them supper. One will spill their milk. The other will fall down. They both will start crying. The noise is too much for the noise in my head. I'll just freak. Before I know it, I'll have hauled off and back-handed one of them. Then I hate myself.

Molly
New York, New York
age 28

My Mind Is Heaving

My mind can't go to any quiet places. It is heaving. Thunder-
bolts are going off in it. I'd love to be participating in life, to
be dancing a dance, but I'm lying here on my bed in my
sweats. I'm lying on the sidelines of life. I feel as if I could
live in this bed and not eat or drink—just dry up.

Bob
Topeka, Kansas
age 37

Alone, at the Temple

There's so much loss and loneliness. My friends and I, we
occupied the whole first bench at temple. Now there's no one
left. They've all gone. For a while I invited some younger
friends to join me, but then they started dying, too. It's too
frightening to ask anyone to join me anymore. I'm afraid
they'll be doomed. I still go to temple, but I sit by myself.

Ben
Providence, Rhode Island
age 80

Staying Organized

My wife has moved out. She's abandoned me—I'm alone with three kids. She's left me for another man. I'm devastated. I don't understand what I did wrong. She says she didn't exist in our relationship—that everything always went my way, that she didn't matter. I don't know that I can keep my life together. I go to work and my mind is rattling, like pebbles in a tin box. I keep going round and round, trying to make lists, to get organized, to make decisions. I think, "If I can only stay organized, I won't lose my mind." I feel so alone. How can I ask for help? How can I tell anyone at work that I'm hurting? I've seen careers ruined because someone asked for help! I just have to struggle through. It's painful and I feel so isolated.

Hal
Anchorage, Alaska
age 42

REFLECTIONS

As I learned about my depression, I began to understand I held my emotions in different parts of my body. For example, sadness got caught in my chest. It made my lungs and chest feel tight. When I was angry, I'd grind my teeth and feel a little nauseous. I began to use my body as a guide to my feelings. In turn, by accepting my feelings, I eased the stress on my body and I felt better.

—Julia

MEDIA VICTIMS

It's so easy to feel victimized by the media. I'm supposed to
live like they do on the sitcoms I see on TV—prosperous and
happy. Or I'm assaulted by voyeuristic programs where people
expose their tragedies for our entertainment. And when
things do go wrong, the media tells me to always be in control. Everything is resolved in half an hour! I'm supposed to
create instant solutions for my problems so that my life can
look perfect again. When I can't act like celluloid heroes do,
I feel like a failure.

Harold
Schenectady, New York
age 39

Half of Me Has Been Cut Away

My wife died. Half of me has been cut away. I'm overwhelmed with depression and worries. I no longer have any
security. Who's going to look out for me? How am I going to
get out and see people? How am I going to eat? I don't have a
good short-term memory, I can't remember if I took my medication. I can't remember if I went to the store or not until I
look for food and there isn't any. I can't just get up and walk
down the street, certainly not in winter.

I should go to a home, but I don't know if I can afford it. I
won't know anybody. It'll all be strange and unfamiliar. What
I really want is to just die like my wife.

Ethan
Springfield, Illinois
age 74

PERFECTIONIST

Whenever I felt sad or insecure I would escalate my perfectionistic needs. That was my form of self-abuse. Nothing about me was good enough. I'd change my clothes fifty times. I had to have everything laid out in the kitchen perfectly, all the knives facing one way in the drawer, all the glasses equally spaced. I couldn't go out at night unless I'd done a series of rituals in a certain order and very precisely. If my toothbrush slipped in my mouth, it meant I hadn't done the exact 82 brush strokes I needed, so I had to start the whole series of rituals over again. Finally it got so bad that my gums were bleeding. When I got to the point that I needed a perfect body and became anorexic, my family finally got me help.

Most people don't believe being a perfectionist is self-abusive. In fact, it's a subtle kind of self-destructive behavior. Because you don't do everything just right you feel like you're going to go crazy.

Susanna
Cranston, Rhode Island
age 20

SURGICAL BLADES

I never wanted to kill myself. Cutting myself was a release. It was a ritual. Because I worked in a hospital, I used surgical blades. They made clean cuts, ones that wouldn't scar much. I would cut myself and watch myself bleed. I used physical pain to relive my emotional pain, but I never felt the physical pain. I would just watch the blood and feel a release, like a medieval bloodletting to relieve bad humors. Sometimes I would go to the hospital. I went to almost every hospital in Philadelphia, but I never told the same story about the cuts on my body.

Sylvia
Cleveland, Ohio
age 39

REFLECTIONS

I had to learn to forgive myself. Every morning I would stand in front of the mirror and say to myself, "You're doing the best you can." At first I couldn't look myself in the face, but slowly I began to talk to myself as if I was a friend. Then I didn't feel so lonely.

—Julia

Sick All the Time

I keep getting sick. The doctor at work says it's nothing life threatening. I get a cold, then flu, then stomach pains, then a pain in my chest, always something. I've been missing a lot of work. I just don't feel good. I wake up in the morning and I don't want to get out of bed. At night I don't want to go to sleep. I don't see any relief to the routine of my life. There's always work and never enough money. I'm tired of it. I just don't feel anything matters any more. And now I'm always getting sick and having to stay home in bed. The doc wants me to talk to a social worker. He says some of my illnesses might be connected to my attitude. I don't want to go see a social worker. I'm not crazy.

Tommy
Boston, Massachusetts
age 41

My Husband Died

For the first year and a half after my husband died I couldn't read a full paragraph at one sitting. I couldn't concentrate. If I stayed still I would be overwhelmed with memories and anguish. I was living in a fog the consistency of cotton candy. Breathing was an effort. I had to repeat to myself all the time, "Keep breathing. Just keep breathing."

When someone you love dies, you die in a way, too. It's three years now, and I feel as if only now I am beginning to think.

Lisa
Columbus, Indiana
age 59

PILLS

I hated the pain of how desperate I felt all the time. I hated it so much that I kept using Percacet and Halcion, Valium, Xanax—any drug I could get a doctor to prescribe, and I had more than one doctor. I would do the rounds, getting each doctor to prescribe what the other wouldn't. I was a prescription-drug addict. At one point I was taking 53 pills a day to keep me from feeling. It was all legitimate, all legal. I had a special drawer where I kept all the pill bottles. They were alphabetically arranged. I was in love with my pills. I loved the colors, the shapes, how they felt in my mouth, the thought of them melting in my stomach. Then, of course, I thought I loved what they did to my body—until I overdosed. That's when I found out that all those drugs were actually depressants—drugs that made me feel more depressed when they wore off.

Alice
Pittsburgh, Pennsylvania
age 34

REFLECTIONS

When I was trying to escape a painful feeling, I would do too much and get tired, then I'd pick a fight with someone I cared about. I'd feel worse after the fight so I'd drink wine to numb my feelings.

—Julia

AFFAIR

When I found out my husband was having an affair, I got so depressed I stopped eating. I lost 17 pounds in one month. I couldn't get to sleep at night. When I lay down my heart would start racing. I felt frantic and very sad. I drank coffee during the day and wine at night. I was medicating myself any way I could. No one had ever taught me how to deal with "heart" things—the loss of love, the rejection. I didn't know what to do with all my sadness and anger.

Sheila
Jackson, Mississippi
age 39

I Drank to Numb My Loneliness

I'm sober now, but I wasn't for years. I drank because I was trying to hide—numb—my loneliness. I was a middle-aged man with no wife, no family. Nothing to look forward to. What difference did it make? Life was hopeless.

At first I never drank until after six in the evening. You know how it is, you say to yourself, "I'll just have a beer to relax. It's been a hard day at work." I'd get kind of numb at the edges, fuzzy. After a couple of years, I started drinking at lunch, too. It helped with the stress of my job. I wasn't drinking much—a couple of beers at night, a beer at lunch. But eventually I started drinking vodka. It has no smell on your breath. I hid it in Diet Coke. I'd start drinking Diet Coke in the morning. I was numb all day. I don't understand why I wasn't fired. I guess no one realized.

For a couple of years I managed OK. I was still able to cook myself some meals, to get up in the morning. Then I began to put on weight. I couldn't be bothered to make a decent meal so I ate anything that came in a bag—bags were easy to open. I stopped combing my hair. I got real disagreeable with everyone. Eventually, I didn't even want to get out of bed. I was afraid I'd run out of something to drink.

Pete
Atlanta, Georgia
age 60

PAYING BILLS

The hardest thing for me to do when I'm depressed is pay the bills.

I never have enough money. Paying the bills always escalates that stress to unbearable proportions. I also feel like such a failure. How come at my age I can't make ends meet? If I was a good person I'd know how to manage my money and live a financially responsible life.

When I look around me—in the magazines, at the movies, on TV—the rest of the world seems to be making enough money to live with everything they need. I must be a loser because I can't afford to live like everyone else seems to.

Matthew

Alexandria, Virginia

age 47

FRIGHTENED

I'm frightened. I'm always anticipating that someone is going
to scream at me, a cop in the street, my boss. I'm sure I'm
going to be held up or get a flat tire at rush hour. Every ache
and pain in my body convinces me I'm going to die of cancer.
I can't sleep. I wake up in the early hours of the morning terrified. I'm either afraid of dying or that the house is going to
be broken into. I have nightmares. I wake up sweating, paralyzed with fear. It's been several weeks now. I think I can't
make it, I can't go through another day and night feeling this
way. I feel beaten up, my body feels as if I've been in a fight.
Nobody seems to understand. After all, in southern California, nobody is supposed to be depressed.

Richard
La Jolla, California
age 52

REFLECTIONS

One day I made two lists: all the things I was scared of and all the things I wasn't scared of. I wrote down even the littlest things. I was scared of the toaster, I wasn't scared of the toast. After a while it was fun and I started laughing. Writing these lists helped me relieve my fears and I discovered a lot about myself.

—Julia

DISCARDED

I feel discarded, as if I don't matter anymore. My kids treat me with tolerance, but I feel like a burden to them. There's no room for older people today. I have a lot to share, but because I can't get around at high speed or I have "old-fashioned" ideas, society pushes me to the fringes, assumes things for me that don't have anything to do with who I am.

I have a lot to contribute, but nobody asks for it. The other day, at the elderly center I go to four days a week, I was sitting in a chair looking out the window, remembering. Well, the social worker comes up to me all in a flap that I wasn't doing anything. They get so nervous when you're not doing anything! Quite forcefully, with this sickly sweet voice, she insists I learn how to crochet. Well, pleeeease, I've never crocheted in my entire life and I'm not going to learn now. I'm a book person; I've been an editor and researcher all my life. Why don't they ask me who I am? Don't I matter?

Teresa
Sioux City, South Dakota
age 79

"Normal" People

I see "normal" people walking and talking and doing "normal" things and I think, "How in God's name are they doing this?"

Phyllis
Chattanooga, Tennessee
age 36

It's Hard to Change

It's easy to stay depressed and stay negative. It's hard to change. Being depressed and negative is familiar. It's what you know. Changing it means dealing with the unknown. It means finding a different way to behave, to relate. How do you know there's anything better than what you already know? When you're depressed you're scared, you suffer anxiety attacks. If you're already scared and anxious, why would you want to go into the unknown?

Carla
Fort Meyers, Florida
age 43

REFLECTIONS

As I learned to identify and bear the feelings of my depression, I began to feel a sense of hope. Perhaps I could be happy again. I made a list of all the things I had loved doing as a young girl. I titled it "Over time, I still can." One of the things was to dance. At 37 I took beginning ballet classes. I wasn't very good, but it made me feel better. The music and concentration took me away from my pain.

—Julia

✳

Look well into thyself; there is a source of strength which will always spring up if thou wilt always look there.
—MARCUS AURELIUS

PART II

WORDS OF HOPE

*

As You Begin
Your Search for
Support and Healing

*

A lifetime of happiness: no man alive could bear it: it would be hell on earth.

—GEORGE BERNARD SHAW, MAN AND SUPERMAN

Life was meant to be lived. . . . One must never, for whatever reason turn his back on life.

—ELEANOR ROOSEVELT, THE AUTOBIOGRAPHY OF ELEANOR ROOSEVELT

A STRAITJACKET OF MISCONCEPTIONS

I think denial is probably the hardest obstacle to overcome with depression. Everything rewards denial. First, depression itself makes you feel broken, sluggish, suffocated, forgotten. You don't care. Your mind doesn't work, so you deny your reality.

Then society has put a straitjacket of misconceptions around depression sufferers. There is a real social stigma because depression brings up so many fears in people. Fears of movie images like *One Flew Over the Cuckoo's Nest*. Fears of the unknown: What's going on inside me? Am I strange?

We don't exactly have national heroes who are admired for their suffering. The people the public look up to are all incredibly competent and high achievers. Where does that leave those of us who don't want to get out of bed in the morning?

When I read the classics in college—Homer, Shakespeare, Hawthorne—there were lots of examples of people in emotional turmoil. In their eras, it seemed as if it was a necessary part of being a complete human being. So, what happened? How come we deny that part of us now?

Brad
Honolulu, Hawaii
age 43

IS THERE SOMEONE INSIDE?

When the psychiatrist asked me to look inside myself and tell him who lived in there, I couldn't find anyone. All there was was a black hole. I panicked. I realized I was no one.

The doctor told me not to worry, I had lots of opportunity to become anyone I wanted to be. He said, "Why don't you imagine a flower pot in that black hole. Fill the pot up with planting soil. Plant a seed in the soil. Don't worry about water or sunlight—I promise they take care of themselves. The only thing you have to do is watch who grows. Someone will grow and you can let her grow any way she wants. She is safe inside you. No one can make her be anything she doesn't want to be." That image gave me hope.

Allegra
Brookline, Massachusetts
age 48

WIFE BEATERS

Every once in a while I'd go nuts. Something would go wrong. There wouldn't be enough money in the bank. Or I'd get hassled at work. I'd lose it. When I'd come home I'd hit my wife. I didn't care how hard I hit her. One day, so that I could hit her, I ripped the baby from her arms and slapped her in the face. Then I threw her across the room. She called the police and I got arrested.

The court sent me to a therapist for evaluation. Part of the program was that I had to meet with a bunch of guys who were wife beaters. You know what? Every one of us, all 15, had been beaten by our parents. Some of us even knew that our parents had been beaten. I realized that I was passing the violence on to my kids. But what really got me was that I was depressed. I felt so hopeless that all I could do was lash out. I hurt my kids because I was so hurt. That was the most terrible realization of all.

Herb
Atlanta, Georgia
age 27

SEXUAL ABUSE

Because I cut myself, my psychiatrist is helping me remember if I was sexually abused as a child.

I thought sexual abuse meant being forced to have actual sex or some sexual activity. Now I know differently. Once, when I was twelve, my mother got mad at me for some-thing—I don't remember what. When my father came home she complained to him about my behavior. He came upstairs just as I was getting out of the shower and took off his belt and started beating me with the metal buckle. He could not stop hitting me. He lost it. I had bloody welts all over me. I will never forget that.

Another time, when I was around the same age, a guy lunged at me in an elevator. He said I had the biggest breasts he'd ever seen. When I told my parents they didn't believe me. They said it never happened. I felt as if my reality didn't exist, as if I didn't exist.

Bebe
Macon, Georgia
age 35

I'm Not a Loser

I lost my job nine months ago. The bank I work for was seized and I was let go. I haven't been able to find work. My wife took a job as a cook. She hated it and quit. We both started drinking heavily. The financial and emotional pressure became too much and she left me. It has been hell. When I go on a job interview and I tell the interviewer what happened I can see him flinch. He thinks I'm a loser. I started to think so, too, until I talked to a friend and he said there are hundreds of thousands of us in this situation. I don't think there's anything wrong with me. I may look like a loser to someone on the outside, but I know I'm not.

Jack
Boston, Massachusetts
age 48

REFLECTIONS

As I practiced telling myself, "I'm doing the best I can," I began to think about the things I did right. At first I couldn't come up with anything. One day I caught myself thinking, "I love my red shoes." I said it out loud. After that, every time I found something I liked about myself I wrote it down so that I could refer to it when I was feeling sad and alone.

—Julia

DEALS

I didn't kill myself, because I had a thin thread of fight in me. My therapist made it safe for me to live, no matter how much pain I was in. He would make deals with me. He would help get me through the weekends and holidays. He would say, "Call me Saturday night and we'll talk for one minute." Then on Saturday night, we'd make a deal for me to call and talk for another minute on Sunday. To me it meant somebody cared, somebody was there for me, somebody was consistent and reliable.

Laura
Rochester, New York
age 33

BAD SEED

For years I was misdiagnosed. As a teenager everyone called me a "bad seed" because I did a lot of pot. It was my way of numbing my mood swings. I found out afterwards that marijuana heightened my depression—it was numbing when I was high, but afterwards I sunk into deep, deep abysses.

In my early twenties I was hospitalized for schizophrenia. It wasn't until I was in my late twenties that I was properly diagnosed for manic-depression. Boy, was that an instant label! Now I was a legitimate nut: a manic-depressive. I hid this new identity, embarrassed, ashamed.

Manic-depression is called bipolar disease because of extreme mood swings. At one end of the pole you're up, or manic, and then you crash to the other end of the pole and are down, or depressed. When I was manic, I felt omnipotent. I believed I could "doctor" myself, that I knew what I needed better than any doctor, that I didn't need help. When I wasn't manic, when I was at the depressed end, I was too pained to do anything or see anyone. I would isolate myself, reinforcing my down feelings of being a bad person.

For three years after my diagnosis, I denied not only the truth of my condition but also support and help. One day, during a down cycle, I was lying on the sofa watching a local TV talk show and they mentioned NDMDA—National Depressive and Manic Depressive Association. They flashed the phone number of the local branch. I'm not sure why, but I wrote it down. About an hour later, I thought, What the hell, I'll give them a call. This man answered who seemed to understand exactly how I was feeling. It took me a while, but I finally went to an NDMDA meeting. Almost instantly, I felt I had finally found somewhere I belonged. Here was hope.

Al
Chicago, Illinois
age 31

WALKING DEPRESSION

There are hundreds of faces to depression. There's chronic depression, acute depression, manic-depression, dysthemia, hypomania, situationally induced depression, and more.

There's walking depression, a chronic condition like walking pneumonia—you feel terrible but you have no acute signs.

I've suffered from walking depression all my life. I think a lot of people do. You know the famous personality-type description? Some people look at life as a half full glass of water, others look at it as half empty? Well, people like me who suffer from walking depression belong in the half empty category.

I never feel enthusiastic about anything. I have very little faith in positive outcomes. I don't believe in myself. I don't trust anyone. I live my life—my job, my dates (if I have any), my friendships—in a fog. I stumble around unable to get very motivated because I'm afraid of what I might run into. Actually, I don't even think I'm afraid of accidents, I just feel too flat to really do anything exciting.

Walking depression lives in your bones. It makes your bones feel like tubes of water—heavy and unstable. I'm always asking myself if it's worth standing up. I'm never sure I have the internal structure to get me through a task. It takes so much effort.

I think there are thousands of people suffering from walking depression. They don't know there's anything wrong with them, because they've always felt the same way.

That's why Prozac is so popular. Finally, there are drugs that clear the fog from your life. With clear vision you feel as if there's more hope, more potential. You're willing to try more. "My God!" you say to yourself after a week on Prozac or Zoloft. "There's a whole world—a whole way of being—I never knew anything about."

Zoe
Charleston, South Carolina
age 32

My Inner Voice

Twelve years ago all I could think about was killing myself. It was horrible. I was afraid to sleep. Afraid to wake up. I spent every day exhausted, drenched in a clammy sweat from fear that I would drive off the road or jump from a building or turn on the car exhaust. I didn't know how to ask for help. I assumed I was a bad person and that I should be dead. Being dead would feel better than being alive.

But inside me there was a shred of a person I'd never met who really wanted to live. I really believe in miracles because that hidden person inside me got me to a doctor. Luckily the doctor recognized that I was severely depressed and got me a psychiatric evaluation.

I began taking medication and seeing a psychiatrist.

Now I know that person inside me very well. The psychiatrist taught me techniques that helped me hear my inner self. They call the techniques cognitive therapy.

Now, whenever I'm hurting or confused, I ask the person inside me what to do. I sit very quietly and try to empty my mind of any judgmental voices. I listen to how I feel when I have an idea. If the idea makes me wince, I know it is not right. The ideas my inside person gives me always feel good, they never make me wince.

I've learned to trust myself and that person inside. I'm really very happy now.

Clara
Baltimore, Maryland
age 25

REFLECTIONS

I had a caring inner voice, too. My voice was more a feeling than a sound. It felt warm somewhere in my lower abdomen, just below my stomach. I also had a voice in my head, which my therapist called "the board of directors" because it was always making rules and criticizing; it felt harsh and metallic. He suggested I fire them! I always try to focus on the warm feeling because I know it will care for me.

—Julia

MY THERAPIST GAVE ME POWER

My therapist cared so much about me, I wanted to live. She was the first person in my life who was there for me. She listened. And she heard. She remembered what I had said and helped me understand the feelings I had. She helped me understand I wasn't crazy—that the feelings I had were real, that other people had them, too.

She made me feel safe. She set limits. Limits that made me feel protected. Some psychiatrists and therapists set limits that make you feel afraid and guilty. She set limits that gave me emotional boundaries. I had to make deals with her that I would call her if I felt suicidal. I had to keep a diary of how I felt and the good things I did for myself. Basically, she gave me goals and targets to focus my boundless emotions on. She gave me the tools to feel I could contain my overwhelming feelings.

But most important, she worked with my depression, not against it. She would say to me, "Let's be depressed. Let's be purposeful. Let's see what this depression has to teach us." It gave me power. I no longer felt ashamed of being depressed. Sometimes I even felt excited.

Trina
Burlington, Vermont
age 27

SPENDING TIME WITH MYSELF

I know that my depression, as long as I admit to it in myself
and am responsible about it, does not affect my decision making. After all, I've been depressed for four years and business
is better than ever.

I always make sure that at some point in the day, if I need
to, I find a way to spend time alone so I can cry or honor my
feelings.

Depression takes energy, energy I could use more produc-
tively.

Martha
St. Louis, Missouri
age 58

TIDAL WAVE

I had this dream. I was standing on the beach. A tidal wave was sweeping toward me. It was massive—a massive wave crested by a rim of fire. I felt tiny. I knew there was no way out. I was about to be overwhelmed.

As the wave hit I decided not to fight it; I decided to go with it, to let it take me. It caught me up, sucked me up to its crest and carried me ashore. I didn't die.

That's when I learned my depression was teaching me not to fight it or try to defeat it. It was teaching me to ride it, to use it, to go to new places in myself and in my life.

Now I consider my depression my ally. Which doesn't mean I'm not afraid. I am. But I own the fear, I ride the fear; the fear doesn't own or ride me. I listen to what it has to tell me.

Harriet
Denver, Colorado
age 40

Writing Makes Me Feel Better

When I think I can't stand it any more I write my feelings down. I have a special pad, you know, like the ones our kids use in school. Now when I feel lonely and sad, I keep myself company with my notebook. I sit in the kitchen and write. In the beginning, I didn't write very much, just things like: "I'm so angry." "I cried for an hour." "I eat a lot of candy, but I wish I didn't." But now I can sit down and write a few pages. It makes me feel better.

Betty
Tulsa, Oklahoma
age 39

REFLECTIONS

Another thing my therapist helped me with was writing in a journal. He encouraged me to write everything and anything I felt. It didn't matter how much—even one word. Sometimes I just wrote the date. When I could, I wrote my feelings. It was very comforting.

—Julia

RECOGNIZING MY FEELINGS

My therapist taught me to recognize "emotional coping patterns"—habits I had developed during my life to protect me from feeling pain.

If somebody said something that reminded me of something painful, my mind would get fuzzy. I would shut down and panic. For example, if my husband got angry and criticized me, he reminded me of my drunk mother screaming at me when I was a kid. Or if I was angry at myself because I'd overdrawn the bank account, I'd lose my temper, then, you know, I'd hit the kids or something. I didn't realize what I was doing. They were knee-jerk reactions, habits I'd been using for years.

Over time my therapist taught me to recognize the shut down, the panic, the violent rage, as patterns I had learned as a child either because I'd seen them at home or because I had needed them to stay emotionally safe. Now I can say to myself, "Aha! That hurts. OK! Pay attention to the hurt. Take time out from what you are doing. Note the feelings. Am I angry? Am I sad? Do I feel desperate? Frightened?"

Slowly I've gained power over my reactions instead of my reactions overpowering me. I've learned to take responsibility for my feelings and I don't hit the kids.

Angela
Grosse Pointe, Michigan
age 29

BOOKS ON TAPE

I like to think I accept the things that come with old age—
fallen arches, lost eyesight. But when I actually began losing
my sight I became severely depressed. I was an avid reader
and I wrote lots of letters. Without my sight I couldn't do any
of the things I loved. I really didn't want to live anymore.

My kids, however, got me books on tape from the Library
of Congress. Now I read a different way, with my ears instead
of my eyes. It saved my life.

I told my friends around the country who have bad eyes
that they can get books on tape from their local libraries.
We've taken it a step further: we've got a whole new way of
communicating with each other. Instead of letters, we send
tapes. Sometimes we exchange books, too. I feel like I'm part
of the world again.

May

Chapel Hill, North Carolina

age 82

Pet

When you're in the hospital for a long time, they should let you bring your pets. I was hospitalized for severe depression for six months. I would have loved to have had my little dog with me to keep me company. My little dog gives me a reason to cope. I get up and do things because I have to take care of him. And he loves me, too.

Hannah
Rochester, Minnesota
age 63

REFLECTIONS

Boy, did I have a lot of "shoulds" and "shouldn'ts." I should be doing this, I should have said that, I shouldn't have said that, I shouldn't have eaten that dessert. I made my life miserable with "shoulds" and "shouldn'ts." I learned to say to myself, "I want to." "I don't want to." After all, it was my life and I was only going to live it once.

—Julia

Financial Security

I'm a very successful lawyer. So is my husband. We have everything public opinion says we're supposed to have: nice house in suburbia, two cars, vacations, designer clothes, kids in private school, a modern high-tech kitchen, you name it.

What we don't have is a happy marriage. My husband never touches me, he never says a nice word to me or the kids.

Why am I willing to stay in my depressing and repressing relationship for the sake of financial security? Because my idea of financial security is not just enough food on the table, but enough clothes—expensive clothes—in my closet. I'm afraid I will be no one without all the trappings, including a husband. Even though I earn a great salary, without my husband's, too, I wouldn't have enough to live the way I do now.

I know I'm miserable, so I've joined a therapy group. They're all professional women like me. I'm trying to find the courage to change my situation, even if it means leaving my husband. I'm not sure walking around as a well-dressed emotional corpse is a compromise I want to make anymore.

Kitty
New Orleans, Louisiana
age 35

OLD LOSSES

I remember realizing how we hold painful memory in our body and mind. I fell in love with this kind and gentle woman after years of being on my own. About six months into this very supportive relationship I became very depressed. I was in terrible emotional pain. I was full of fear. Luckily, I was in group therapy so I had a place to talk safely about my feelings. Slowly, I came to understand that I was terrified of loss. I was afraid of losing the kind person who had come into my life.

But why was I so terrified? I was terrified because I had lost a woman whom I loved very much as a child. I was six when my grandmother suddenly died. My grandmother lived with us and took care of me when my parents worked. She used to walk me to school every day.

One day I came home and she wasn't there. She'd died. But, because I was a child, no one paid attention to my grief. They just told me she had gone to join grandpa and was very happy. But I felt abandoned and betrayed. As a small child, I had no idea what to do with the feelings. I decided, as a little boy, that women I loved could just disappear. I never trusted women again. Years later, when I felt the safety and security of the same kind of gentle love I had known with my grandmother, all the old grief came up, all the old feelings of fear and loss.

Because these feelings had been simmering inside me for so long, they were, I guess, concentrated, more intense even than when I was a little boy. I really felt very desperate reliving all that old sorrow and anger. But once I relived the grief and stopped denying it, I no longer felt depressed.

Dave
Minneapolis, Minnesota
age 55

I Did the Best I Could

I had to learn to recognize the language I used about myself. Instead of saying to myself, "Boy, did you blow it. You are such a screw up," I learned to say, "Well, that didn't work. That's OK. You did the best you could. Now you know better."

When I was a kid I couldn't make mistakes. Now I know that mistakes are experiences and experiences are the road to wisdom. We certainly aren't born with all the answers, so if we can't make any mistakes how are we supposed to learn in life?

Perfection is a very scary thing to be burdened with. I felt much better when I realized that I didn't have to be perfect, that no one was going to punish me for not being perfect, and especially that I didn't have to punish myself.

It took a lot of practice to learn to say nice things to myself. I got the hang of it the day I realized nice things weren't said to me as a child. I had this memory of being criticized by my teacher for not knowing my multiplication tables. I think it was the 9s. I thought, Well, if I can memorize the 9s, I can memorize saying nice things about myself. So, just like in school, I'd repeat "I'm doing the best I can" to myself. For example, I'd do it as I made myself a cup of coffee—the whistle of the hot-water kettle was like the school bell. Briiiiing! Say your "be nice to yourself" tables!

George
Louisville, Kentucky
age 41

REFLECTIONS

I used to hide all my painful memories in an imaginary closet in my mind. By age 36, the closet was overflowing and I was spending a lot of energy keeping its door shut. One day I realized how much effort it was taking to hide from these feelings. So, with the help of my therapist, I went to the closet and pulled the memories out one by one until the closet was empty. I always thought a huge beast of a memory would jump out and terrify me, but all the memories turned out to be smaller than me—scary but not overwhelming. Emptying that closet freed me up!

—Julia

VERBAL VIRTUOSO

I was a successful politician. I am now the most productive lawyer in my firm. I'm famous, I handle huge case loads and make bundles of money. When I was "on" politically and when I'm "on" now as a litigator, I'm the best. I'm a verbal virtuoso.

I'm also what's called hypomanic—a milder form of manic-depression. I have mood swings, but not so acute I'm a social risk. I'll be "on" or extremely competent for weeks, then I'll crash with a bout of depression—either an illness, usually bronchitis, or a period of paralyzing melancholy.

No one suspects my behavior because society admires and encourages extreme productivity. The greater my output, the more I'm praised and rewarded. This admiration pulls me out of my depressive states, then I pursue the admiration to avoid the depressions.

The only thing between me and a megalomaniacal white-collar criminal such as Ivan Boesky or Michael Milken is my secretary. Laura covers for me. She runs interference for my insane schemes. I could have made a fool out of myself if she hadn't intercepted all communications. I believe I can do anything when I'm "on." I can work for 19 hours a day. But when I'm not "on," I'm at home staring at the ceiling, incapable of even picking up the phone or making myself a meal. Then Laura tells people I'm out of town or some other important plausible excuse. She's so good at managing my life she has everyone fooled.

I like to say I got lucky. Laura needed an operation and was out of the office for several weeks. It was my good fortune that her absence depressed me instead of turning me "on." I went home and did the usual—ceiling stared. Without Laura to cover for me, my office tracked me down in two days. One thing led to another and one of the partners got me to a doctor. I was diagnosed, put on Lithium, and I began therapy. For several months I thought I knew more than the doctors, but I'm smart enough now to feel the difference when I take my medication and when I don't.

For the first time in my life, I'm beginning to find some balance. That's making me much happier.

Dimitri
New York, New York
age 50

SURVIVAL INSTINCT

I think that inside most of us there's a survival instinct, no matter how bad life gets. I think I knew I was going to lose it.

I got to a therapist, I think, as a last desperate act. I don't remember deciding to go or even finding out the name of a doctor, but somehow I got to one.

I went to a psycho-pharmacologist. Thank goodness I did. She explained I was suffering from depression and that depression was easily treated. She recommended medication and that I speak with a social worker who specialized in depression, particularly depression in women. Did you know that twice as many women as men are depressed?

I took the antidepressant medication for six months and spoke with the social worker. Both doctors encouraged me to exercise, so I did that, too. After six months I felt fine. I went off the medication and I've never been depressed since.

Petra
Kansas City, Kansas
age 34

ALLOWING MYSELF TO BE DEPRESSED

I've suffered from depression all my life. I can remember as a teenager waking up in the morning not wanting to get out of bed, with this horrible oily feeling of dread weighing me down into the sheets.

For years I fought my depression. I found every way I could to overcome it, beat it, control it, push it away. I'm a very wealthy woman. With my financial resources I could try a lot of different things. Believe you me, there wasn't a doctor I didn't see or program I didn't try to gain control over my depression. I'd go to each one for a little while and then when I didn't feel better I'd move on to the next person or program.

I remember waking up one morning when I was 32 and saying to myself, "Sarah, you're addicted to doctors and programs. You need to stop running away. You need to live your depression."

I looked for a doctor who would allow me to be depressed, who would actively help me engage in my pain, not just sit there and listen. I wanted to live the pain, to find the memories that triggered painful feelings and bear them. By bearing the pain I learned to move with it and through it. I learned that trying to beat or overcome depression was just another way of pursuing failure and remaining depressed. Depression is a signal that something is wrong. If you try to ignore the signal you won't get to know what's wrong. Now, whenever I feel depressed, I ask myself, "What do I have to learn?" I have put my depression to use; it no longer has power over me.

Sarah
Chicago, Illinois
age 46

REFLECTIONS

Admitting my depression was an important step to getting well. I had to accept myself—my weaknesses and my strengths. I had to give myself permission to be what I was—depressed. Only then did I begin to trust in my abilities and judgment. I realized that there were many things I was doing very well despite being depressed. Just getting up in the morning was an accomplishment sometimes. All of us do something well—even though we have trouble recognizing it. Sometimes it's a very little thing.

—Julia

DEPRESSION PASSES

Depression passes. In the meantime I have to make sure I am doing everything I can to get the support and care I need to manage the rough road of depression. Am I getting enough sunlight? Am I eating regularly? What am I eating? Am I sleeping? Am I overworking? Am I drinking too much? Have I shared with my wife how I feel? Am I expressing my feelings or am I denying them and acting irritable? Should I call my psychologist? Do I need an antidepressant?

Robert
Portland, Maine
age 38

MY STRENGTH AND VOICE

It was through my depression that I learned to define my own strength and voice. By bearing the pain of my depression I learned how much strength of character I had. If I could bear the pain of depression I could cope with the challenges of life.

My depression has also brought clarity to my life, whether through escaping it or being humbled by it. It has taught me spirituality, a sense of awe and humbleness. Through the humbleness I have learned to love and accept other people. Love and acceptance have taught me not to be afraid.

In turn, by not being afraid to be alive, I am no longer as depressed.

Amanda
Salt Lake City, Utah
age 47

STRONG AT THE BROKEN PLACES

You won't believe this, but I think my depression is one of the best things that has happened to me. People and life have more meaning to me.

Because I have been on the edge, have looked death in the face, and have endured great mental suffering, I have an appreciation for life that people who haven't suffered might not have.

All those crosses I've had to bear have made me stronger. I know I've got endurance. I can recognize and enjoy the good moments because I've certainly known the hellish ones.

Once I admitted I suffered from depression I joined a support group. I wasn't alone anymore. I met lots of wonderful people. Face it, if you let them, difficulties bring people together.

Belonging to a group has given me hope. I have to be hopeful or I'd be sitting in a corner staring at the wall.

Irene
Woodland, Washington
age 36

PAIN AND SUFFERING

I think you have to understand pain and suffering. Pain and suffering are part of life. They are the measure for joy and happiness. How could you know what happiness is if you didn't have suffering to compare it with?

But you have to admit to pain and suffering the same way you admit to joy and happiness. It has to be as OK to say, "I feel lousy today," as it is to say, "I feel great today."

Most of us have been taught that we can't admit to pain and suffering, so we bear it in silence. We make ourselves alone in our pain and suffering. In fact, it should be the opposite. If we need companionship, we need it in our pain and suffering. We can bear being alone in our joy and happiness.

Janet
San Francisco, California
age 55

REFLECTIONS

I felt so alone in my depression. It was so hard in the sense of sorrow and lack of self-worth to think that anyone wants to be with us or that anyone can help. I found courage in history—knowing that famous people like Alexander the Great, Abraham Lincoln, Virginia Woolf, and Mozart had suffered from depression for years. In fact, many famous people have used depression as a source of inspiration.

My experience with depression has changed my life—for the better.

—Julia

✳

How you regard depression depends on how you experience it. Because, by its very nature, it is associated with endings, and because each ending involves starting over, depression is itself a new beginning.

—FREDERIC FLACH, THE SECRET STRENGTH OF DEPRESSION

PART III

THE EXPERIENCE OF HEALING

*

As You Work Toward Emotional Well-being

*

Man's main task in life is to give birth to himself, to become . . . what he potentially is.

—ERICH FROMM, MAN FOR HIMSELF

If I am not for myself, who will be for me? If I am for myself alone, what am I? If not now, when?

—HILLEL, THE TALMUD

WHAT EARLIER GENERATIONS KNEW

Pain is not part of our culture's reality. Earlier generations knew pain and suffering were part of life and that they could survive it. Our culture and generation doesn't know it, so we don't have confidence in who we are.

Pain and suffering are part of life, just as joy is.

George

Cambridge, Massachusetts

age 35

EMOTIONAL FREEDOM

You can't take on joy until you are emotionally free. Emotional freedom is accepting the pain and the happiness. Freedom is allowing all of you—and all of you is the pain and the happiness, the imperfections and the perfections.

If you are denying part of yourself, hiding from the parts you don't like, then you can't be free because you are burdened, even imprisoned by the need to hide from yourself.

For me to find all of myself I had to allow a full-blown depression. I had to feel and become intimate with all the parts of myself I didn't like or felt others didn't like.

But I couldn't work through this painful process alone. No one should try to go through that process alone. You need support, a therapist, a support group, good friends, a priest, a counselor, people who care about you and don't judge you.

Chris
Des Moines, Iowa
age 31

KEEPING MYSELF COMPANY

When my mind gets dense like clay and I have rocks inside my chest, I sit down and write whatever comes out of my pencil.

It's usually about how I feel—just plain words—or about things I would like to do or a nice thing someone said to me. I just let my thoughts pour out onto the page without punctuation or caring if it makes any sense. I only tell myself that it has to be positive. When negative thoughts come to mind, I have a little conversation with myself, as if I were a friend talking to me. I talk myself out of the dark places. It's a way of keeping myself company and I don't feel so alone.

Tom
Cincinnati, Ohio
age 30

Talking Made Me Feel Real

The month I found out my husband was having an affair, I found out my father had prostate cancer, my brother had hepatitis B, my sister, who was seven months pregnant, had a blood clot in her groin, and my mother had breast cancer. It was too much. I felt helpless. My body felt as if my legs were cement. I couldn't move. I couldn't make a decision. I couldn't stop crying.

I'll never forget those months. I think if I hadn't talked to everyone I met during that time I would have gone crazy. Truly, I talked to everyone. I'm a flight attendant. Lots of different people come into my life in a day. I told everyone my problems. I told the pilots, the other flight attendants, the cleanup crews, the duty-free agents, the room service guys in the hotels I stayed in, the passengers that came into the galley during flights, everyone. If I hadn't talked I would have exploded. Talking made me feel real. It affirmed my feelings when people sympathized. I felt less alone and overwhelmed.

Cynthia
San Jose, California
age 36

REFLECTIONS

As I got better and learned to bear my feelings, I tried to remember to be good to myself. For example, I took a hot bath or made myself a nice meal. Sometimes it was as simple as patting my dog or brushing my hair. Being good to myself was not easy. It took practice. One time I simply wrote over and over again—like the way I used to practice spelling words—"I will be good to myself!" Writing and rewriting affirmations helps.

—Julia

WALKING THROUGH THE STORM

Exercise is what got me through the hard times. I started walking to work during the week. On weekends I'd go for long walks around the city or I'd do laps around the reservoir. I got a little cassette player/radio and listened to music or the news. When I found out about the tapes of books that I could rent from the library, my walks were even better.

Walking took me away from the four walls of my apartment and from the repetitious voices that haunted my head. I found out years later that exercise of a certain intensity and duration releases endorphins—natural chemicals that have a positive effect on your moods. I guess, without realizing it, I was helping to heal my depression by exercising.

Mike

Jamaica Plain, Massachusetts

age 47

SAFETY

It was scary going to the hospital. But it was scarier staying home. I needed a place to be safe, to be with people who understood my anguish. I wasn't suicidal, but I couldn't cope at home anymore. I wasn't sleeping. I was terrified, wracked by anxiety attacks. I was so exhausted from the terror and sleeplessness that I couldn't even comb my hair or make a sandwich. I just sat paralyzed day after day. I voluntarily committed myself for a set amount of days, which meant that I could leave at the end of the designated time. But I still felt afraid I would never get out. Even knowing that it would take legal action to change my voluntary commitment to an involuntary commitment didn't totally comfort me. And, despite the really supportive staff, I felt ashamed for a couple of days. I didn't like standing in line with everyone else for my medication and I hated being checked on every half hour at night.

But after a while I got used to the change in routine. I began to feel cared for and secure. It was deeply relieving to be with lots of people who felt the way I did. Some of them were sicker than me, and that gave me perspective and hope. If they could cope and get better, so could I.

I'm really glad I went to the hospital. I think it is one of the most important things I did for my recovery.

Audrey

Saratoga, Florida

age 27

ALWAYS LISTEN IF THEY SAY THEY WANT TO DIE

My husband didn't take me seriously. I can remember lying in bed at night mumbling, "I just want to die." He would tell me I was being melodramatic. He'd say, "It makes me nervous to hear you talk like that. Besides, you have so much to live for!"

One day all I could think about was dying. I was going to go to the basement and kill myself with drugs, alcohol, and a plastic bag. I was terrified—of myself, of living, of dying. Somewhere in the back of my mind a little voice kept echoing the TV ad of the Samaritans, a suicide prevention group. I called them. They were the first step to getting help for myself.

Now I tell everyone who will listen, "Never ignore a person—even a small kid—who says he or she wants to die. It could be too late."

Arlene
Boston, Massachusetts
age 32

HEALTH COSTS

Almost every person in my depression support group used to have chronic physical illnesses before they were treated for depression. But tell that to an insurance program!

Everyone in our group readily admits they were always in the doctor's office being treated for this or that—some real illnesses, some imaginary illnesses. Insurance would pay for those visits. The companies they worked for would pay for it, too, in lost production costs. Ironically, now that we are aware of our depression, we don't go to the doctor anymore and we rarely miss work. We do have psychotherapy and, in some cases, medication costs, but we are no longer bleeding the corporations and insurance companies for time and medical expenses.

You'd think insurance companies and corporations would get wise. Instead, there are no adequate benefits for mental health. Now does that make sense? I think it would be more financially efficient to invest in an employee's emotional well-being because it affects his or her physical well-being. It's like the old proverb: a stitch in time saves nine.

Vincent
Charleston, West Virginia
age 55

REFLECTIONS

I didn't use just psychotherapy or medications to get well. Over the years I learned to meditate, get regular exercise, write poetry, eat well, and pay attention to not getting overtired. I learned visualization and relaxation techniques and alternative healing practices. I joined groups and took workshops so that I could be with people. I found it helpful to make a list of things I could do to help myself.

—Julia

REPROGRAMMING THE MIND

I don't believe a pill is the only treatment for depression. If you have bipolar disease—manic-depression—you almost always have to take medication. But in my case, antidepressant drugs were only the first answer.

I had spent years being sad and not living up to my potential. Then I got a new job, moved to a new city, and found a new doctor. He pointed out that I might be suffering from chronic low-grade depression. He put me on Zoloft, a Prozac-type drug. I felt better than I'd felt in years. I finally got some initiative.

I started reading about depression. I read that depressive behavior is inherited and that addiction and victimization are characteristic of depression. I began thinking about and looking into my family history. I realized that most of my family were heavy drinkers. So I joined Al-Anon, the support group for children of alcoholics.

At Al-Anon meetings I learned about emotional abuse and alcoholic behavior and how to recognize the ways I emotionally protected myself. I got curious, it's as simple as that. "OK!" I thought. "Maybe there's something else I can' do besides take a pill."

In the psychology section of the library I found some books on cognitive therapy. A cognitive therapist teaches you about depressive behavior as well as tools and techniques to unlearn that behavior.

For four years I've been working with a cognitive therapist

that I found through our county mental health service. I'm not chronically depressed anymore and I don't take the antidepressant. There is no question that medication gave me the strength to undertake my "retraining," but, coming from a family of addicts, it's too easy to give my happiness away to a pill. Giving a pill the responsibility for my well-being is another way of saying, "I'm not capable of being happy." As I've learned in cognitive therapy, pills can be another way of perpetuating depressive victimization.

Berenice
Burlington, Vermont
age 36

ECT

When my husband died, I slipped into a serious depression. I can't remember ever being depressed before. It happened very quickly. I gave up on life. I didn't see any purpose. It seemed that without my husband there was no reason to live; his death took half my being.

I started to die. I just sat at home in a chair and wasted away. I didn't eat. I didn't get up. I didn't change my clothes.

One of my friends sent a geriatric social worker—a person trained in caring for the elderly—to see me. She took me to a special doctor. Everyday I was dying a little more. Finally, I went to the hospital and had ECT treatments.

ECT is electroconvulsive therapy. The doctors give you an anesthetic so you don't feel anything and then they apply an electric shock to your system. After three treatments I felt immensely better. Now I know that ECT has a higher success rate for treating severe depression in the elderly than any other treatment.

After I felt better, my children wanted me to come live with them. I didn't want to live with my children. At 67, I'm selfish enough to want my own way. I want to be with my own generation, people who understand the issues I live with. Living with my children would have been a burden on me and on them. So I live in a home with lots of people my age.

Bertha
New London, Connecticut
age 67

RECOGNIZING WARNING SIGNALS

There is absolutely no question that, if I pay attention, my body and mind will let me know I'm heading for a depressive period. I begin to hold a lot of tension in my neck and shoulders. I lose any interest in sex. I withdraw from my wife and kids and become grumpy, short-tempered. I notice that I eat foods, like chocolate cake, that I usually don't eat. I doubt myself at work.

Because I'm beginning to feel bad about myself, it's hard for me to pay attention to the warning signals. But I try. I try to ease up on myself, to not be self-critical, to remind myself of the things I do well, even if it's one very trivial thing such as bouncing a basketball. I also try to do nice things for myself. I'll make sure I take time off on the weekend instead of getting frantic about all the chores I have at home. I'll take a long, hot bath. I'll go to the movies with the kids. I'll reach out for support by going to church or having a long lunch with one of my friends.

Bob
Lansing, Michigan
age 44

FORGIVENESS

I really believe that my mind can make me feel either better or worse. Whenever I'm down, I always notice that I'm very critical of myself. I try and say nice things to myself and forgive myself and I begin to feel better.

Carl
Fredericksburg, Virginia
age 60

REFLECTIONS

I learned to recognize when a situation <u>triggered</u> a painful memory. I would either get very angry and defensive or my mind would turn into concrete—gray and hard. Once I recognized these reactions, I was free to begin to <u>identify the feelings</u> behind them. The feelings, in turn, created images that allowed me to recognize the painful memory and heal it. Step-by-step, I soothed the old pains.

—Julia

AN EMOTIONAL JACKHAMMER

It's not easy to let go of old feelings. They can get buried deep inside, like sharp stones wedged into the soft tissues of your body by layers of concrete. Sometimes you have to take an emotional jackhammer to loosen them up before you can dig them out. I call that loosening "transition"—transition to emotional well-being, free of the weight of old painful memories and hurt.

Transition is difficult and demanding work because acknowledging feelings is hard to do. It's like taking out a splinter. It hurts. But once the splinter is out, the pain's over and you're free. Letting go of old feelings is the same thing— getting them out frees you.

Once you reach the other side of the transition, you can look back and see how bleak it was before. You can also see how much stronger you've become now that you're no longer being weighed down by all those sharp stones.

The only difference between loosening old feelings and digging out splinters is that you can't always loosen old feelings alone. Sometimes you need help.

Jeff
Seattle, Washington
age 30

Monsters for Tea

I have an imaginary game I play with myself. I invite my monsters to have tea with me. Whenever fear and anxiety come to visit and try to drag me into the dark depths of despair, I stop everything I'm doing and say to them (of course, I say this inside myself because that is where I am feeling the panic), "Sit down at the table with me. Let's talk!" Then, in my mind I pull up three chairs to an imaginary table set with an imaginary tea service and I ask my monsters to join me. Once they are sitting down I say, "OK, you two. What's up. I'm listening."

By transforming my fears and anxieties into physical monsters I give them a tangible form. They take on properties I can understand: they're my size and about the age of my grandchildren so I feel secure. I can relate to them. I can see their weaknesses, so I know how to manage their moods. By sitting them at the table with me, they become equals, and by conversing with them I feel strong enough to gain control of my own emotional life.

Mary
St. Louis, Missouri
age 62

THE RICH ARE NOT DIFFERENT

I'm from a very wealthy family. People think being rich insulates you from everything. It's true that money protects you from the despair of economic hardship. What people don't understand is that being very wealthy is also isolating. Everybody was afraid of us. I always was made to feel different. I was so lonely.

Everyone thought I had the perfect life, because I had so much. Instead I had an awful life. I was physically abused by a nanny for years. I would scream and cry in the children's wing of our house, but my mother never heard or came and protected me because she lived in a cloud of prescription drugs on the other side of the house.

I started taking drugs as a teenager. My mother had drawers full of them. I'd steal several bottles. She never noticed she had so many. The drugs numbed the trauma of my loneliness and fear. By my senior year in boarding school I was in a mental institution being wrapped in ice packs to treat my withdrawal from cocaine. All my family could say to me was that I had disgraced the family name and that the only reason the school would take me back was because my father made a huge contribution. All I wanted was for someone to hold me and love me. Instead I repeated my senior year feeling humiliated.

As soon as I graduated I became a cocaine addict again. The second time I was hospitalized for cocaine addiction I was over eighteen, legally an adult. I was able to develop a relationship with my doctors independent of my parents. I learned that I suffered from a trauma-induced depression, that I had been emotionally and physically abused for most of my life. When the doctor said I had been fundamentally deprived of vital nurturing, all I could think of was, "Maybe that's what they mean by 'poor little rich kid.'" The truth is, emotional and physical abuse takes place in all socioeconomic worlds, nothing protects you against it.

                                                    Susan
                                      Wilmington, Delaware
                                                   age 29

CHANGING FRIENDS

Some of my friends were intolerant of my depression. Every time I was with them I felt guilty. They always said something that made me feel guilty. Perhaps they'd say, "For heaven's sake, Mike, cheer up, you're making us feel horrible." Or, "What you have to do is get up and do something." Of course, I was so depressed that I couldn't even think of what I might want to do. I'd feel like a failure because I couldn't do any-thing. On top of it, I'd feel responsible for my friends' feelings.

Other friends showed concern. They'd talk with me about my feelings and invite me to the movies. Slowly I learned to spend time with friends who supported me.

I began to see less and less of the old friends who made me feel bad. At first it was scary to stop seeing the old friends. Then I realized that hanging out with them was a way of staying depressed because I was used to feeling bad.

It took courage to change my friends. It was tricky. My old friends were angry. They made me feel guilty. One friend said I'd gotten strange and aloof. I had to really pay attention not to get bullied into feeling I'd done something wrong. I had to remember I wanted to feel better and that spending time with friends who didn't criticize me felt good.

Craig
Scottsdale, Arizona
age 32

REFLECTIONS

Getting better means taking risks. The first risks I took were physical, like starting ballet classes at age 37. Then I took emotional ones. I began expressing my thoughts. I joined a support group. I made new friends. If there is something good for you that feels emotionally risky, try writing it down. Sometimes seeing it in print gives you courage.

—Julia

WORDS ARE MY COMPANIONS

The strange thing is the more I wrote, the more I wanted to read. Words became my friends. It was scary to go to a book-store, but I did. I stood for a whole hour doing nothing but focusing on books that had words that made me feel better. I realized that there are a lot of people who feel sad and lonely the way I do.

Suddenly, I understood that I could find those people. So I went back to the bookstore and looked at books that had words about how to find people like me.

Betty
Tulsa, Oklahoma
age 39

EMOTIONAL SUPPORT

It's really hard to remember to be good to myself. When I get in the rough times the first thing I do is forget to take care of myself. I start to feel that everything is my fault, that I can't do anything right, that I'm a victim and helpless.

I'm in a hard time now. I'm getting a divorce. I was unhappily married for years. My husband would get in bed with the kids, my son and my daughter. He'd tell the kids he was cold and that we'd had a fight and I'd thrown him out of bed. Because I had an uncle who used to get in bed with me when I was little, at first I thought it was normal. But I read a lot and I learned that what my husband was doing was incest.

I got involved in a sexual abuse support group. The name of the group was listed in the back of a book on sex abuse that I found in the library. Eventually I tried to get my husband to go to the group with me, but he said I was crazy and denied he ever got in bed with the kids. Sometimes I thought I was crazy, but the group supported me and I didn't feel so alone.

The group helped me find a job and a lawyer. Now I'm in court suing for divorce and custody of the kids. I have to relive all those sad years and drag up all the details. I feel a loss of self. I feel all the helplessness I felt as a child and as I watched what happened to my children.

But I've learned to go back to the basics. I ask myself daily: Am I getting enough sleep? Did I eat right? How can I take care of myself? Now I know that taking care of myself is the best way I can take care of my kids.

Elizabeth
Salem, Oregon
age 38

SOMEONE CARES ABOUT ME

I live in the projects. My neighbors heard my baby crying for a long time. When I didn't open the door they got the superintendent to let them in. I'd passed out on the floor.

I hadn't been eating because I was too tired always to make myself any food. I wasn't sleeping because I'd wake up in the middle of the night with nightmares. I was afraid of the nightmares so I was afraid to sleep. I finally passed out from exhaustion and hunger.

In the hospital the doctors wanted me to talk to a shrink or someone like that. "Not me!" I said. "Those people mess with your head. They do strange tricks on your mind and make you crazy. For all I know they'll put me away in a nut house for the rest of my life." Anyway, this shrink came and talked to me and gave me some medication, an antidepressant. I took the medicine because I figured if I took the pills I wouldn't have to talk to a shrink again and I'd get to go home. The pills made me feel a lot better. Once I was feeling better, I felt a little more courageous, so I went and spent an hour with the shrink. It wasn't bad. I felt OK when I left his office. Now I go once a week. I go so I can get my pills, but I think I'm beginning to go because it feels good that someone cares about me. I don't feel so alone anymore.

Charlene
Boston, Massachusetts
age 24

GOOD FRIENDS

I need to surround myself with people who support my feelings. To feel better you have to learn to care about yourself.
My feelings of hopelessness, helplessness, fear, sadness, and
anger that obsess me when I'm depressed are very real, very
much a part of me. I need to care about those feelings, too. If
my friends disregard my feelings by saying things like, "You
don't need to feel that way," or "Snap out of it," I can't feel
OK about being depressed. If I feel it's wrong to be depressed,
then I'm just compounding my bad feelings about myself and
repressing my reality. If I'm going to get better and take care
of myself, I have to accept how I feel and be around people
who can accept my feelings, too.

Margerie
Nashville, Tennessee
age 45

REFLECTIONS

After a while I was able to recognize habits, conversations, and environments that made me uncomfortable, as well as people who made me feel that way, too. I made notes in my journal about where and when I felt bad. Slowly I began to accept that I could change my circumstances—that I didn't need to see people who hurt me or do things that hurt me.

—Julia

MEDICATION?

You'd be surprised how easily some doctors will prescribe medication. I was a prescription pill addict. I took anything I could get a doctor to prescribe. I made up lots of symptoms, but all the symptoms involved anxiety. Sometimes I'd go to the emergency ward with imaginary heart attacks—imaginary because there was really nothing wrong with me, but I believed there was. I had to believe it—if I could convince myself, I could convince the doctor on call. The doctor would always give me a sedative. I loved the blissful feeling I'd get from the drugs. Whenever something happened—talking with my mother, getting stuck in traffic, even burning the toast—I took another pill. I was spending all my money on the drugs.

One day I overdosed. I woke up in the hospital. I went nuts. I wanted pills to make me feel less scared. By overdosing I'd given my secret away.

I joined a drug program, and I found out that all the drugs I had been taking were compounding my depression. The psychopharmacologist—that's a doctor who specializes in drug treatment—explained that I was suffering from depression and that the drugs I had been self-medicating with were depressants as well as addictive. Now I take an antidepressant, one nonaddictive pill. When a feeling seems more than I can handle alone, I have a therapist to help me. I'm learning new ways to cope with my fear and anxiety. By the way, I'm also saving money.

Lois
Omaha, Nebraska
age 26

PARTS THAT DON'T WORK

When my arthritis set in, it was very depressing. I couldn't get around anymore. I couldn't do the simple things in life, like pick up a tea pot. At first I just sat at home and stared at the TV. I felt sorry for myself and very lonely. Then I thought, "There's nothing I can do about this. It's part of getting old to have parts that don't work. You can give up your life to it or you can find a way to live in partnership with your aches and pains."

That's when I knew that living alone was no longer a good idea. Every time I tried to do anything I was reminded of my disabilities. It was too huge a struggle to stay positive. I wanted to get away from my depression and I wanted physical and emotional security.

Now that I live in a home with other people, I've gotten away from my loneliness and I have the capacity to get around to lots of activities in the outside world—things I couldn't do at home. Getting outside to a concert, museum, or some other activity makes life worthwhile.

Zachary
Fulton, Missouri
age 70

Turning Off the TV

One night I stopped watching TV—it was too depressing. I don't know why, but that evening I was stunned by the amount of violence and negativity in the news stories. All I was seeing and hearing was death, economic disaster, famine, rape. There was a rapid pace to the stories, as if it was exciting to tell this kind of news. I began to feel so depressed that I turned off the TV. I also felt angry—there isn't anything exciting about tragedy.

It was lonely in the beginning because the TV had kept me company, but I'm not nearly as frightened as I used to be. I'm learning to do new things, like read, go to the local church for bingo, volunteer at the homeless shelter. In fact, I'm less lonely than I was. Now I know lots of people whom I didn't know when I was staying home staring at the TV screen—I've got lots of people to talk to and share with.

Pearl
Cleveland, Ohio
age 66

COMPANIONSHIP

I went to my church and found a free counseling group. The people there have stories similar to mine. We help each other. We talk about how we feel. I'm amazed that so many people feel like me. I thought I was alone.

Jodie
Cleveland, Ohio
age 64

REACHING OUT

I've learned that hurting myself is a way of coping with emotional pain. Whenever I feel like hurting myself, I call a friend. I don't make the friend feel responsible. I don't tell him or her to distract me because I feel like hurting myself. I just find a friend to do something with, like go to the movies. The most I'll say to them is, "I'm feeling a little sad, let's go do something."

Marietta
Baltimore, Maryland
age 30

REFLECTIONS

Reaching out can be scary, but I learned that if I reached out and the person didn't respond it was not because there was something wrong with me. It was because he or she was afraid. I crossed out the phone numbers of people who didn't respond or criticized me, and I wrote down the numbers of people who were supportive.

—Julia

SURVIVING VIETNAM

The memories of Vietnam won't go away. For a long time I drank and did drugs to escape them. Then, 10 years ago, after my car accident paralyzed me from the waist down, I couldn't numb myself with booze any more. I began to live with daily suicide thoughts. I kept thinking: What right do I have to be alive? How come I'm here? How come my buddies aren't? How come I get to live in a wheel chair?

Anyway, in the VA hospital they told me I was depressed. I'm suffering from PTSD—posttraumatic stress disorder. I joined a support group of other vets. Fifty percent of the guys in the group are physically handicapped in some way. A lot of them, like me, are handicapped because of self-induced accidents that happened after they got home: drunk driving, suicide attempts, death-defying feats like jumping off cliffs—crazy stuff. I don't think too many people get it. They don't know how pissed off Vietnam vets are—they've got a lot of anger.

We talk about the hell of coming home after a year in combat. What do you think it feels like to be scared to death in the dark jungles off in the country one minute and then, only hours later, on the tarmac of some big-city airport back home, standing there wondering whether you're dead or alive, while some dude says to you, "Hey, change into your civvies so no one knows you're a soldier." Fuck man, you've been risking your life for your country for thirteen months, now suddenly everyone's ashamed of you. Makes you feel really great!

You come home, right? You think you're safe, right? No way! You're still getting hit! In Vietnam you were scared to die. Now you're scared to be alive because no one likes who you've been for a year. Your reality doesn't count. You don't count. Hell, I killed 'cause they told me to, not 'cause I wanted to.

Group has helped a lot. It's taught me that it's OK to cry. You got to cry; you got to mourn the loss of so much and so many. I counsel other vets. I tell them to cry. We hold each other. We were there for each other in the jungle; we can be here for each other now, too.

Gary
Boston, Massachusetts
age 48

FOOD FOR HAPPINESS

We so often overlook the obvious when we hurt emotionally. It never occurred to me to be conscious of what I ate. Then a nutritionist pointed out to me that, very often, when someone is suffering from depression, they eat foods that feel emotionally good rather than self-nourishing.

The predominant feeling when I start having an emotional crisis is to try to escape. I don't want to be in my body or in my life. That is a scary feeling. So I start eating a lot of foods that ground me, that weigh me down: "white" and "brown" foods—foods that have the color of the moods I'm in.

White and brown foods—bread, cheese, meat, sugar, chocolate, coffee, fried foods, fast foods—block energy, and have few or no minerals or B vitamins. Minerals and B vitamins are important elements your body needs to cope with depression. Also, although white and brown food may make you feel temporarily better with the rush they provide to your system, when their effect wears off, they leave you feeling worse than before. Basically they're drugs. And they're fattening, so their long-term effect is to compound the feelings of low self-esteem in the body so prevalent in depression.

The nutritionist suggested that I eat vegetables and fruit at every meal and that I drink a lot of water to keep my system moving. I have to admit it took some discipline, but it made a huge difference in how I felt. Now I eat fruit instead of candy between meals, and I make sure lunch, as often as possible, is a big salad. I also take B-complex vitamin capsules once a day, but only the ones without sugar additives.

Harold

Las Vegas, Nevada

age 36

S.A.D.

Every fall, I like to think of myself as a lizard stretched out on a rock in the bright sun getting warm. It's very comforting.

I used to dread the fall. When the leaves dropped, my mood would, too. I'd see the first leaves on the ground and I'd panic. I'd start to be sucked into a black vacuum. I couldn't work; I wouldn't want to wake up; and I'd start putting on weight. I couldn't help it. Every fall I'd start this cycle that would last all winter. As soon as the days got longer and the green leaves started on the trees, I'd start to emerge again. Don't laugh, but I often wished I was a bear so I could just go hibernate until spring. It seemed very sensible to me, and a lot less stressful than trying to maintain a regular life.

Then I read in the newspaper about S.A.D—seasonal affective disorder. There, in black and white print, were my symptoms. According to the article, something called the pineal gland in my brain secretes a hormone called melatonin. This hormone, which is associated with depression, is stimulated by darkness. The article explained that when the days get shorter and cloudy in the fall and winter, some people's pineal glands secrete too much melatonin. This makes these people slow down, want to sleep, and get depressed. What I needed was light, because light tells the pineal gland to decrease melatonin secretion.

At first I thought I could go to a tanning salon and get ultraviolet light. It turns out that that's bad for you. You have to get the light in the early morning and early evening in order to affect the pineal gland. It's called phototherapy. Phototherapy is easy to get. I found out from my local mental health organization where to go.

By the way, the reason I think of myself as a lizard is because a lizard's pineal gland is close to its skull, so light has an immediate effect.

Susan
Minneapolis, Minnesota
age 31

ACOA

Both my parents were alcoholics. I didn't exactly get a lot of consistent love and support growing up. I never really knew when I came home from school whether my mother would be passed out on the couch. And Dad spent most of his nights at the bar. When he came home he either got in a fight with my mother and hit her or he passed out on the couch, too. I spent most of my childhood hiding my family from my friends and trying not to go home.

When my father died, a friend of Mom's got her into an alcohol abuse program at the local hospital, and she stopped drinking. That's when we all learned that our family suffered from depression. The program wasn't just for the drinker, it was also for the whole family. They explained to us—my brother, my sister, my mom, and me—that the whole family compensates for the behavior of the family member who is suffering from depression. What that means is the whole family learns to live according to the needs of the depressed member.

Well, both Mom and Dad were depressed and they drank to numb the pain of their depression. That meant that we kids learned to relate to each other and the world in terms of our depressed parents. In other words, we learned to see the world through the eyes of depression. As a result, we were suffering from depression, too.

My husband and I don't have much money, so I couldn't afford a therapist. The hospital suggested I join their program for ACOAs—Adult Children of Alcoholics—or Al-Anon, a twelve-step support program. These programs are free. I go to Al-Anon once a week. It's been a great help. What I think has helped the most is learning that there are lots of other people who have depression in their families, too, and that I don't have to hide anymore.

Tricia
Bismarck, North Dakota
age 38

REFLECTIONS

Exploring the events in my life and the lives of my parents and grand-parents provided abundant clues to some of the mysteries of my despair. The more I knew, the more I felt able to do something about my life.

—Julia

ALTERNATIVE HELP

I think sometimes that people who treat depression—internists, psychologists, psychiatrists, social workers—believe there is only one way to heal it. I don't think there is only one answer. In my case there were many techniques that helped me cope with and heal my depression.

For starters, I worked with my depression instead of trying to ignore or overcome it. I tried to understand what it was all about and what thoughts or experiences made me feel more or less depressed and hopeless. I kept a journal of my mood swings. It included things like the time of day and year, what I was thinking, whether it was raining, whether I was sick or well, what sensations I felt in my body. This helped me feel less helpless when my painful feelings became overwhelming. After a while I noticed a pattern to my mood swings. In turn, the pattern—a chart of early warning signs—helped me look out for and be prepared for risky times so that I wouldn't get hit out of the blue.

Then I used alternative techniques such as meditation and visualization. I learned a meditation technique in a stress program the local high school offered that helped me calm my anxiety. The visualization practice, which I learned from a popular book, helped me balance my negative thoughts with positive images of myself.

I really don't think I could have felt better without combining these techniques with more traditional therapies.

Pete

Syracuse, New York

age 32

CHANGING THERAPISTS

Finding the right therapist is not necessarily an easy task. I was with the wrong therapist for my first three years of therapy. When I began to suspect he might be the wrong person, I felt very guilty. I kept thinking there was something wrong with me. I kept denying my instincts.

One day I was talking with a friend who was in therapy, but with another therapist. After listening to my complaints, my friend said that my therapist was always telling me what I should or shouldn't be doing and always trying to impress me with his clients and social life. My friend asked me how I felt when I left my therapist's office. I realized that I usually felt worse than when I arrived. My friend told me she usually felt better.

I finally got the courage to change when I understood that it was my money I was spending—I was the customer buying a service. I wouldn't spend my money on food I didn't like, so why was I spending it on a person who made me feel bad?

As a member of an HMO—Health Maintenance Organization—I didn't have many therapists to choose from. But I picked someone whom I liked as a person, not just because he had credentials and said he knew what he was doing. I think people with other kinds of insurance, who can choose from a bigger pool, should interview therapists. They can give their business to a person who respects them and makes them feel valuable. Certainly no one should ever stay one minute in the office of a therapist who makes any kind of sexual innuendo or gesture.

Sal
Corpus Christi, Texas
age 33

GIFTS FROM THE PAST

My parents always told me I was adopted. In their loving and generous way they also told me that if I ever wanted to find my birth mother they would help me.

When I was twenty I began to suffer severe depressions. The therapist who was treating me at that time asked my parents if they knew any personal details about my birth mother. They told the doctor and me that they knew my mother had been a drug user and she had left me in a garbage can.

Perhaps I always felt I had been unwanted and that my feelings of worthlessness came from that original abandonment.

Anyway, I came to believe that in order to recover from depression I would have to find my birth mother. I knew that in order to be whole in my life and to have a goal for the future I would have to confront the past. To know who I was—or wasn't—I would have to know where I came from.

It took almost five years, but we found her. She was living in a dilapidated trailer on the outskirts of a small town in Arizona. I could tell she'd tried to clean up before I got there, but her whole place smelled like stale alcohol. We had a short visit; she wasn't sober.

I've never seen her since, and she's never tried to find me. But I've learned a lot about myself. I know I may have inherited depression from her. I know I am a different person than she is, with different values. I know I had the strength to endure the very painful truth of my mother, what she did, and who she is. I know I'm lucky to have had the chance to grow up with my adoptive parents. And I know I was right— by confronting the past, I have made possible my future.

Frances
Bayshore, New York
age 28

REFLECTIONS

"Don't ever regret making a mistake." I'd repeat this to myself whenever something didn't work out. "If I was supposed to know everything, I'd have been born an adult." Then I'd try and discover what my mistake taught me.

—Julia

NEW PLACES

I'm learning to say what doesn't feel good, instead of trying to deny the painful feelings of hurt, anger, and sadness. I'm moving into new places of being with myself, acknowledging the feelings and letting them flow through me instead of holding onto them and burying them. It's hard to make the changes—even though, when I do, I feel better.

In the new place the pain will pass, whereas in the old place the pain just sat there and ate at me. But it's hard to remember that the pain will pass. It's hard to remember that I can bear the pain while it lasts without getting drunk—it's hard to remember to recognize how I feel and to separate the feelings from needing to go out and get self-destructive.

That's when I remember to call someone in my support group or a friend who's been to AA, too. That's when it's really important to remind myself that I am not alone.

Kate

Omaha, Nebraska

age 50

ONE STEP AT A TIME

Depression is overwhelming. It swamps you—usually when you are least expecting it. You need to remind yourself of what you can do to get through the crisis.

The first thing I try to remind myself is not to look at the big picture. When I'm depressed I tend to worry about the big picture, the issues I can't control. I work myself into a tizzy about my financial future, my health, whether my grown children and grandchildren are in danger, whether my house is going to be broken into, all the chores I haven't done in the house, whether my wife is going to have an accident. I self-abuse with anxiety about things that haven't happened. To counteract this bad habit I say to myself, "Earl, small tasks, small steps, one at a time. You can only manage the immediate. If you waste your energy worrying about the future you'll ignore the immediate, and it's only the present you have any control over."

Then I find small tasks that I can accomplish and—most important—that I like doing. I'll prune my lemon trees. I'll putter around in the garage, maybe even wash the car. I'll carve an animal for my grandson. Once I've accomplished them, I stop and congratulate myself for a job well done.

Earl

Phoenix, Arizona

age 57

SURVIVAL LESSONS

Finding a depression support group has had a healing effect. I no longer feel isolated or that I'm different. In my support group there are living examples of people coping with the same symptoms I have. I'm awed by their courage. They prove that you can survive. They've taught me how to forgive myself and how to accept the benefits of medication. They've shown me how to be patient; how to pace myself so my mood swings won't run away with me; that learning to live with depression involves making mistakes and mistakes are OK to make.

Most important, I'm no longer alone. I've learned about happiness—there are people like me, lots of people like me, holding down jobs, living their lives, people who care I'm alive.

Ruth
Chapel Hill, North Carolina
age 29

Positive Image

When I realized I had no idea who I was—no one was there when I looked inside myself—my psychiatrist gave me the image of a seed growing in a pot. I was to imagine the pot planted with a sprouting seed inside me. I was to let this seed grow any way I wanted it to. Whatever—whoever—grew would be safe from danger because it was tucked away inside me. This image gave me hope and courage through the years of my recovery.

As I recovered, the growing plant—the budding me—became my secret treasure. This hidden me could do anything she wanted without fearing someone would hurt her.

Now, eight years later, there's a vast overgrown garden where the pot and little sprout once were. I love it—her. The garden is much too big for anyone to do anything to it. It—she—makes me feel wonderful, safe, strong, and capable.

It's amazing how much healing one positive image can cause!

Allegra
Brookline, Massachusetts
age 48

REFLECTIONS

I have discovered over the years that almost everyone I know has been depressed to one degree or another at some point in their life. I could fill this page with names of people who are surviving as I am. All of us need to congratulate ourselves for bearing our pain and learning the tools we need to cope with it. We are very courageous.

—Julia

✻

I think I shall always remember this black period with a kind of joy, with a pride and faith and deep affection that I could not at the time have believed possible, for it was during this time that I somehow survived defeat and lived my life through to a first completion, and through the struggle, suffering, and labor of my own life came to share those qualities in the lives of people all around me.

—THOMAS WOLFE,
THE AUTOBIOGRAPHY OF AN AMERICAN NOVELIST

PART IV

CONCERNED VOICES

✳

The Feelings of
Those Who Love Us,
Work with Us,
Arc Associated with Us

✳

There is no point in treating a depressed person as though she were just feeling sad, saying, There now, hang on, you'll get over it. Sadness is more or less like a head cold—with patience, it passes. Depression is like cancer.

—BARBARA KINGSOLVER, THE BEAN TREES

DEPRESSION HAPPENS TO OTHER PEOPLE

It never occurred to me that my husband might be depressed. Depression was not something that happened to the people we spend time with. You know what I mean. It's like people say, "It's OK to hear people talk about depression on the talk shows, but I certainly wouldn't want a depressed person as a neighbor or a depressed man marrying my daughter."

My husband did ask me once if I thought he was crazy. I knew he wasn't crazy, I just didn't think about depression. I wish I had now, he wouldn't be dead.

I'm not sure it would have made a difference if I had known he was depressed. He never would have admitted it. Depression just wasn't acceptable—not in our social economic world. You know, where I come from, if you're feeling sorry for yourself, everyone says, "Go out and do something. Buy a new dress. Play a round of golf."

I guess you could say I've learned the hard way. I now know depression affects everyone. I know you can inherit it. I know there are drugs that can alleviate the despair. I know there are all kinds of therapists that can talk to you about your feelings. I even know that group support, exercise, meditation, acupuncture, massage, certain foods—all help heal depression.

I know all this now, but it's a little late, isn't it? What I know won't bring my husband back. I needed that information when he was sick.

Marge
Lincoln, Nebraska
age 53

ALL IN THE FAMILY

It was very scary when I was ten and my sister was thirteen. Our father had abandoned us when we were very little; we lived with our mom. My sister would get so angry. She'd lose it. She'd lash out at my mother. Sometimes she'd throw things—chairs, books. She'd even kick and hit my mother. My mother tried to explain to me that my sister was depressed and in a lot of emotional pain. Mom always tried to assure me that my sister was seeing a therapist and would get better. But it kept happening. I would feel so helpless. I was afraid one day my sister would kill my mom. I'd lie in bed at night and thrash around like my sister, only I'd be mad at my father for abandoning us and divorcing my mother. I thought my mom needed help. I learned to be a very good girl so that my mom wouldn't have any more problems.

It took about four years. My sister started taking antidepressants and then, over time, with the help of the therapist and lots of love and patience from Mom, she started being less angry.

Mom got us all in family therapy together. I learned a lot about depression. It affects the whole family even if only one member behaves depressed. In therapy I admitted to being very angry at my sister. I also had to deal with my own depressive behavior. It wasn't easy always being a good little girl—it puts a lot of pressure on you.

Jennifer
Des Moines, Iowa
age 22

Your Brother's Kinda Nuts

I'm very proud of my brother. Tim is brilliant. He has taken responsibility for his condition and has the benefit of medication and therapy. He has a prosperous career and a stable life. He's a successful financial adviser for a well-known firm, and he's also a published poet. But for several years I never knew when my husband and I would get a call from the police because he'd been arrested for dangerous behavior as a result of a manic break.

Manic-depression often manifests itself for the first time in males during their mid-twenties. Tim was twenty-four when he had his first episode. He said he heard a mystical voice that instructed him to make a clearing in the woods a mile from the small town we live in so that a religious shrine could be built in honor of whatever deity had spoken to him. A neighbor saw Tim chopping at the trees and called the police.

The police arrested Tim and took him to our local jail. Luckily, we live in a small town, so they knew who Tim was. They called my husband and me. Can you imagine what would have happened if Tim had lived in a big city?

I remember one of the policemen saying, "Look, Tim's kinda nuts. He needs special care." It's very very scary to hear someone say your brother is "kinda nuts"—no matter what he's done. You get angry. You don't want to admit it.

Lily
Millbrook, New York
age 37

Self-Doubt Hell

God, the fragile self-esteem of teenagers—it's devastating. I don't think I know of a teenager who doesn't live to one degree or another in what I call "self-doubt hell" for no other reason than that he or she is a teenager. Add to that cauldron broken homes, experiencing or witnessing emotional or physical abuse, misdiagnosed learning disabilities, alcoholic parents, teenage pregnancy, drug use, neighborhood crime. And how about all the violence and hopelessness in TV news and the movies?

As an adult I find life pretty sad a lot of the time. Imagine what it's like when you're a teenager and you can't find a safe place to be? When the future seems mostly hopeless?

I think a lot of teenagers act out to relieve the pressure of this despair. Five thousand adolescents commit suicide every year and approximately four hundred thousand attempt to kill themselves. Suicide is the third biggest killer of teenagers. What does that tell you? It tells you there's rampant depression and despair.

As a high school teacher I can't afford to be ignorant about depression. Sadly, a lot of my fellow teachers are. I'm afraid that parents don't know much about teenage depression either. The kid that's acting out is usually accused of having a "bad attitude" and regarded as a disciplinary problem. What those kids need—what teenagers need—is empathy and a source of self-respect.

Dan

Lynn, Massachusetts

age 46

REFLECTIONS

I think witnessing other people's pain—especially if we love them—is as hard as bearing our own. Witnessing other people's suffering makes us vulnerable and helpless; it reminds us of our own unhealed wounds. So often we just want the sufferer to go away. Other times we want to rush in and take over their lives. I have discovered that the more I bear my own pain, the more I can bear someone else's.

—Julia

SUICIDE

My husband committed suicide. He jumped in front of a sub-
way train. For six months before his death, he had come
home sadder and sadder. He kept saying the office was going
to kill him. At first he was angry with everyone—all of us,
too. He complained about everything. Everything was wrong:
his secretary was slow, I didn't have dinner on time, our son's
grades weren't good enough, our daughter dressed wrong. We
were terrified of his sudden outrages. Then he stopped talking. Sometimes he would groan and hang his head. "I can't
keep this up. I don't know what they want of me," he'd mum-
ble into his hands. I suggested he talk to someone, a therapist, a clergyman. He couldn't believe I'd suggested such a
thing. He made me promise I'd never tell anyone he was so
desperate. He said he'd never hold another decent job again
if anyone knew he felt so depressed.

Then one day he didn't come home. He was dead. I blame
myself. I keep thinking: If I'd only not listened to him. I wish
I'd insisted he see a doctor. But I was afraid he was right. I
was afraid he might lose his job. Now I know he was wrong.
If he had seen a doctor, I believe he would be alive today
because he would have gotten help. I know I did the best I
could, but I just wish I had known better. I don't think he'd
have lost his job. I think that was just a fear he had because
he was so depressed. I think people now know that depression is controllable and almost always curable.

Blanche
Washington, D.C.
age 57

LEARNING DISABILITIES

There is not enough acknowledgment in schools today about the relationship between learning disabilities and depression in children and adolescents. I have three children with depression. It's possible that they're depressed because depression runs in both my husband's family and my family, but it's also possible that my children's depressions are linked to the self-esteem issues present in their scholastic difficulties.

My oldest was in sixth grade before anyone suspected he had a disability. During Don's first years in school he was referred to as everything from "dumb" to "lazy." He dreaded going to school and eventually began to avoid doing his work.

It wasn't until my youngest, Sarah, was in nursery school and a smart teacher picked up on her disability that we began to suspect something might be going on with Don. As it turned out, all three of my children have learning problems.

Even though we now know the obstacles our children are having to contend with and we have moved them to special schools with special tutoring, their difficulties aren't over. They're different, and to many people they're still dumb. For the two boys, the emotional bruising they've suffered during all the years of being unable to meet the demands of unsympathetic teachers and classmates may never heal. For Sarah, she says, "I feel as if I'm going to school with a huge scar across my face."

Children and families with learning disabilities need special support and understanding about the hardships of being

different. And parents, doctors, teachers—everyone needs to
be on the lookout for the emotional despair of children who
don't fit into the norm.

Gladys
Northampton, Massachusetts
age 43

Job Blues

When you know something is wrong with an employee, you have to respect his or her privacy, but you also have to protect your business.

I have one employee whom I suspect of being depressed. He tries too hard. He always makes excuses for his work and is quick with apologies. He's moody. He's either overly conscientious and solicitous or distant and noncommunicative. He needs a great deal of reassurance. In other words, he takes a lot of personal attention. I try to let him know his work is valued, the way I would any employee, but it doesn't seem to put him at ease.

He always does a good job, so I can't complain. But I run a small division. His mood swings have a certain effect. I can never overlook his need for reassurance or the possibility that one day his behavior will disrupt the office. When that happens I'll have to decide whether to invade his privacy and suggest he use the counseling opportunities through our EAP [Employee Assistance Program], or to let him go. For his sake I wish he knew he could do an even better job if he'd get some help.

Deborah
Milwaukee, Wisconsin
age 47

MISDIAGNOSIS

My grandfather was always energetic. He had a great sense of humor. He loved to do things with all his grandchildren. For instance, he taught us all to drive. But when our grandmother died, Grandpa fell apart. First he cried for months, then he didn't want to get out of his chair. He sort of lost all will to live. His doctor said he was suffering from acute depression. But Grandpa had high blood pressure, so he couldn't take antidepressants. They tried having a psychiatrist talk with him, but he was too depressed to talk or listen. The only hope Grandpa had was ECT, electroconvulsive therapy.

I had seen horrible movies about shock treatment. I argued with my family that Grandpa shouldn't be submitted to that. But, like in a lot of movies, the things I had seen on the screen don't happen in certified hospitals. Grandpa was put into a light sleep before he had the shock treatment, so he felt nothing.

I hated visiting him in the hospital after the treatment. He would be sitting in a chair drooling as if he didn't have a mind left. But then he'd perk right up. The doctor explained that Grandpa's passivity after treatment was the body's reaction to the shock—it was a form of having the body rest. After six treatments, Grandpa was almost his old self again.

Nancy
Wilmington, Delaware
age 33

MY DAUGHTER'S STRUGGLE

When my daughter was suffering from depression she said to me, "Mom, I feel like I'm going crazy." I panicked. I thought: I've got to make it better for this kid. I was terrified of her feelings.

Then I thought: I value the darkness in myself. It has taught me a lot. It has strengthened me. I can't take her pain onto myself. She needs to bear it. I need to acknowledge her feelings and remember that her pain is her growth. Her emotional struggles are very valuable.

I needed to listen to her and allow her her experience. I needed to hold her and support her, but I didn't need to deny her or fix her. Unfortunately, if you slip into emotional darkness, our society says "Don't do that!" or "That's your problem, I don't want any part of it!"

There's a stigma against emotional struggle and depression. As a society we are in denial of difficulty. No wonder we drink so much and are so violent.

If emotional pain is a natural part of life and we deny it, then we are denying a part of ourselves, and that must be unbearable. If we can't admit it is unbearable, we compound the problem and the only escape is to numb ourselves with something—sex, violence, drugs, drink, shopping, etc.

I didn't want that for my kid. I want her to know how to live her darkness as well as her happiness. I want her to be complete, to live a full life.

Charlotte
Lenox, Massachusetts
age 42

REFLECTIONS

Today, when the voices of depression start clamoring, I don't tell them to be quiet. I listen. I believe the quickest way through the darkness is to give in to it, to use it for what it is, or else it will, like a hungry child, shriek at you until it drives you to distraction. I know from repeated experience that if I pay sincere attention, I will learn a vital lesson and heal—albeit painfully—an old sore. I have come, over the years, to respect depression.

I also believe that almost all of us have a memory of someone or something that gives us hope. For me it was my memory of Italian passion. For one friend it was as simple as a hair ribbon. The good feelings attached to those memories have tremendous power to act—if we let them—as a raft and carry us to safety. These feelings will probably float on sadness because they are memories and we miss them. But don't overlook their goodness. Search for moments—even milliseconds—that remind you of the comfort you once felt. Goodness is slow off the starting line, but once it gets going it's hard to stop.

Try not to deny yourself your depression or hide it from yourself and those who can help. You have a right to be depressed because of your personal story and because you are human.

Speak your truth so that people who want to help can hear you. Depend on this book to help you gain courage. On the following pages are different ways to be heard and enlist support.

Remember, you are not alone.

—Julia

✳

We also discover that depression has its own angel, a guiding spirit whose job it is to carry the soul away to its remote places where it finds unique insight and enjoys a special vision.

—THOMAS MOORE, CARE OF THE SOUL

PART V

SEEKING
HELP

✳

There Are Many People
Who Care and Who
Are Ready to Help

✳

First Steps and Emergencies • Support Groups

and Therapy • Recommended Readings

There is perhaps no more effective way to relieve psychic pain than to be in contact with another human being who understands what you are going through and can communicate such understandings to you.

—FREDERIC FLACH, RESILIENCE

FIRST STEPS
AND EMERGENCIES

There are many people who care. Even so, getting help can feel overwhelming.

It is not easy to pick up the phone and speak to a stranger about personal feelings, especially if you feel ashamed. It may seem too great an effort to leave the house and walk into a store or library in search of a book that will help you feel better.

I have tried to simplify the task as much as possible. On the following pages are some suggestions on what to do, whom to call, and where to get information to guide and support you.

In some cases it may be necessary for you to find local phone numbers for the agencies in your area. In other cases you may have a better idea than the one printed. I have left the blank spaces and pages for you to write whatever you need.

Remember, this is your book and you can do what you want with it. Write down notes, feelings, or any other information you want to include in this section. Everything is important to the process of getting help.

If You Feel Like You Want to Die

Please call at least one of the following numbers:

Operator: 0 Ask for the suicide hotline

Police: 911

Local hospital: Ask for the emergency ward

YOU ARE NOT ALONE. YOU ARE IMPORTANT.

SOMEONE CARES. I KNOW.

I THOUGHT NO ONE CARED. SOMEONE DID CARE, VERY MUCH.

YOU MATTER. PLEASE CALL.

THANK YOU FOR MAKING THE CALL.

SEEKING HELP   161

You May Not Be Feeling Suicidal, But You May Be Having a Lot of Death-related Thoughts

Please call at least one of the following numbers:

<u>Operator:</u> 0 Ask for the suicide hotline

<u>Police:</u> 911

<u>Local hospital:</u> Ask for the emergency ward

If You Feel Like Hurting Yourself, Hurting Others, or Someone Is Hurting or Has Hurt You

Please call one of the numbers listed in the previous lists.

No matter how you are feeling right now, you do not deserve to be hurt. You deserve to be treated with love, respect, and kindness.

I KNOW IT IS NOT EASY TO MAKE THESE CALLS.

IT WILL TAKE COURAGE TO PICK UP THE PHONE AND TELL SOMEONE.

ANYONE SEEKING HELP IS COURAGEOUS.

THANK YOU FOR YOUR COURAGE.

If You Feel Depressed

If you are feeling depressed—lonely, afraid, angry, worthless, filled with despair, anxious, paranoid—remember, you are not alone. Please reach out to someone who can support you.

There are many ways to find support and professional guidance.

There are people whom you already know who can help you:

Friend:

Friend:

Personal doctor:

Priest, rabbi, minister:

Family member:

Family member:

There are people who can help you though you may not know them. They are listed in your telephone book. Look in the White Pages under "D" for local depression support groups.

White Pages:

Also listed in the White Pages are state and local government agencies that provide help. These listings are usually in the back section of the White Pages and are colored blue. "Mental Health Agencies" and "Mayor's Hotlines" are some of the headings to look for.

SUPPORT GROUPS
AND THERAPY

There are a number of national organizations that can provide you with immediate support at the local level. The two most prominent are listed here:

National Depressive and Manic Depressive Association

NDMDA is a national organization that has about 250 support groups across America. NDMDA will put you in touch with resources and help in your local area.

Call: (312) 642-0049

Fax: (312) 642-7243

Write: NDMDA
730 N. Franklin Street,
Suite 501
Chicago, IL 60610

Local group number:

Thoughts and feelings:

National Alliance for the Mentally Ill

NAMI is a self-help advocacy organization for people with serious mental illness and for their parents, children, spouses, siblings, and friends. It currently has more than 800 affiliates across the country. Contact NAMI and someone will put you in touch with local help.

Call: (800) 950-6264

Fax: (703) 524-9094

Write: NAMI
2101 Wilson Blvd.,
Suite 302
Arlington, VA 22201

Local group number:

Thoughts and feelings:

MAKING PHONE CALLS IS A BIG EFFORT.

I AM GRATEFUL TO EVERYONE IN THIS BOOK—
ALL OF WHOM CALLED FOR HELP.

THANK YOU FOR YOUR EFFORT AND
COURAGE.

There are other national organizations that provide support at a local level:

Alcoholics Anonymous

AA is a voluntary, nonprofessional, 12-step organization for people who wish to attain and maintain sobriety. Local meetings are held regularly and give members a chance to provide support.

Call: (212) 870-3400;
for the hearing impaired and the blind, TT4:870-3199

Write: Alcoholics Anonymous
        P.O. Box 459
        Grand Central Station
        New York, NY 10163

Local number:

Thoughts and feelings:

Al-Anon, Al-Anon (ACOA), and Alateen

Al-Anon is a fellowship of relatives and friends of alcoholics. Al-Anon (ACOA) is part of Al-Anon and is for adult children of alcoholics. Alateen is also part of Al-Anon and is designed for younger relatives and friends of alcoholics. They all follow the 12-step tradition and hold local support meetings.

<u>Call:</u>   (800) 344-2666

<u>Write:</u>   Al-Anon Family
             Group Headquarters, Inc.
             P.O. Box 862
             Midtown Station
             New York, NY
             10018-0862

<u>Local number:</u>

<u>Thoughts and feelings:</u>

A *note:* AA, Al-Anon, and Alateen can be supportive for alcoholic-related and substance-abuse-related depression. Being in the company of similar people reminds us we need not be alone. However, most AA-associated programs do not encourage the use of any antidepressant or antianxiety medication, which can be vital to saving lives.

A number of professional organizations can supply you with referrals to qualified therapists. These include the following:

American Psychiatric Association

The American Psychiatric Association is a professional organization for psychiatrists. Callers are referred to an APA branch in their state. When they call that number, they will then be referred to one or more practitioners in the area or to a mental health center.

Call: (202) 682-6220

Write: American Psychiatric
Association
1400 K Street N.W.
Washington, DC 20005

Thoughts and feelings:

American Psychological Association

The APA is a professional organization for psychologists. APA refers callers to an APA state psychological association. A caller's name and phone number are taken. A referral coordinator returns the call and provides names of psychologists and mental health centers in the area.

Call: (202) 336-5800

Write: American Psychological
        Association
        750 1st St. N.E.
        Washington, DC 20002

Thoughts and feelings:

Center for Cognitive Therapy

The Center for Cognitive Therapy has a referral list of cognitive therapists around the country. The center defines cognitive therapy as short-term help, usually 12 weeks, that focuses on current emotional problems.

Call: (215) 898-4100

Write: Center for
        Cognitive Therapy
        University of Pennsylvania
        Room 754
        The Science Center
        3600 Market St.
        Philadelphia, PA 19104-2648

Thoughts and feelings:

National Mental Health Association

The National Mental Health Association refers callers to its local affiliate chapter, which in turn helps to choose an appropriate therapist.

Call: (703) 684-7722

Write: National Mental
Health Association
1021 Prince St.
Alexandria, VA 22314

Thoughts and feelings:

National Association of Social Workers

NASW provides the names of social worker members in a caller's area.

Call: (800) 638-8799 and ask for Clinical Register's Office

Write: National Association
        of Social Workers
        Suite 700
        750 1st St. N.E.
        Washington, DC 20002

Thoughts and feelings:

IT MAY NOT BE EASY FOR YOU TO CONTACT THESE ORGANIZATIONS.

YOU HAVE TO HAVE PATIENCE, BECAUSE THEY WILL BE REFERRING YOU TO OTHER PARTIES.

BUT PLEASE MAKE THE EFFORT. THANK YOU FOR THAT EFFORT.

RECOMMENDED
READINGS

Books can be of tremendous help in gaining insight and information. The first six books listed here may be especially useful to you in the early stages of your journey through depression.

To Start

Overcoming Depression, by Demitri Papolos, M.D., and Janice Papolos (HarperCollins: New York, 1992), provides up-to-date information on medical, scientific, and therapeutic aspects of depression. Particularly useful is its discussion on insurance coverage.

Darkness Visible, by William Styron (Random House: New York, 1990), is a short, moving account of the brilliant writer's struggle with depression.

How to Survive the Loss of a Love, by Melba Colgrove, Harold H. Bloomfield, and Peter McWilliams (Bantam: New York, 1991), is a small, comforting book on how to recover from a loss.

Moodswings, by Ronald R. Fieve, M.D. (Bantam: New York, 1989), is a lively account of new diagnostic and drug treatments for depression, particularly for manic-depression.

Feeling Good, by David Burns, M.D. (Signet: New York, 1980), provides an excellent account of how depression can be dealt with through cognitive therapy.

The Consumer's Guide to Psychotherapy, by Jack Engler and Daniel Goleman (Fireside: New York, 1992), is a large book that contains guidance about how to pick a therapist and the difference between various kinds of therapy.

How to Cope with Depression: A Complete Guide for You and Your Family, by J. Raymond DePaulo, Jr., M.D., and Keith Russell Ablow, M.D. (Fawcett Crest, a division of Ballantine: New York, 1989), is a highly readable, comprehensive and supportive guide to the experience of depression.

In addition, the following books may be useful to you:

The Courage to Heal, by Ellen Bass and Laura Davis (HarperPerennial: New York, 1992). A groundbreaking book for victims of childhood abuse.

Minding the Body, Mending the Mind, by Joan Borysenko with Larry Rothstein (Addison-Wesley: Reading, Mass., 1987). An important book on the mind–body connection and the power of healing.

Forgiveness, by Robin Casarjian (Bantam: New York, 1992). A loving book that helps heal the past through forgiveness.

The Depression Workbook, by Mary Ellen Copeland (New Harbinger Publications: Oakland, Calif., 1992). A useful workbook for depression sufferers.

Companion Through the Darkness, by Stephanie Ericsson (HarperCollins: New York, 1993). A touching guide for those in grief.

Resilience, by Frederic Flach, M.D. (Fawcett: New York, 1988). A humane and hopeful book that offers a two-step process as an antidote for times of stress and crises.

Rickie, by Frederic Flach, M.D. (Ballantine: New York, 1990). An extraordinary real-life story of a young girl's misdiagnosis and her courageous fight for health told by her psychiatrist father.

The Secret Strength of Depression, by Frederic Flach, M.D. (Lippincott: Philadelphia, 1974). A readable and empathetic book explaining depression, its causes and symptoms, including practical examples and insights for using depression for personal growth.

Creative Visualization, by Shakti Gawain (Bantam: New York, 1982). A helpful book for learning to visualize a healthy life.

The Good News About Depression, by Mark S. Gold (Bantam: New York, 1988). An informative book on medical treatment about depression.

The Stormy Search for the Self, by Christina Grof and Stanislav Grof (Jeremy P. Tarcher: Los Angeles, 1990). A fascinating discussion of how spiritual emergencies can be transformational.

Silencing the Self, by Dana Crowley Jack (Harvard University Press: Cambridge, Mass., 1991). A pioneering theoretical discussion about women and depression.

The Grief Recovery Handbook, by John W. James and Frank Cherry (HarperPerennial: New York, 1989). A step-by-step program for moving beyond loss.

Women's Growth in Connection, by Judith V. Jordon et al. (Guilford Press: New York, 1991). A feminist examination of psychological theory and practice.

Full Catastrophe Living, by Jon Kabat-Zinn (Delacorte: New York, 1991). A practical, highly readable book on using the mind and body for emotional and physical well-being.

Witness to the Fire, by Linda Schierse Leonard (Shambhala: Boston, 1990). An intellectual book linking the lives and works of famous writers with the stories of individuals to offer hope for recovery from addiction.

Women in Therapy, by Harriet G. Lerner (Harper & Row: New York, 1988). A compilation of essays that challenge traditional notions of female psychology.

When Feeling Bad Is Good, by Ellen McGrath (Henry Holt: New York, 1992). An innovative program for women on how to transform "healthy" depression into growth and power.

The Stress Solution, by Lyle Miller and Alma Dell Smith with Larry Rothstein (Pocket Books: New York, 1993). A groundbreaking, comprehensive guide to dealing with the many dimensions of stress.

Care of the Soul, by Thomas Moore (HarperCollins: New York, 1992). A powerful book that shows how spirituality and nurturing the soul add meaning to modern life.

Illuminations, by Stephen C. Paul (HarperCollins: San Francisco, 1991). A small, supportive, beautifully illustrated book of lyrical insights.

Contagious Emotions, by Martin Podell (Pocket Books: New York, 1992). A useful explanation of the impact of depression on others and relationships.

Here Comes the Sun, by Gale F. Rossellini and Mark Worden (Hazelden Foundation: Center City, Minn., 1987). A general book on depression.

Solitude, by Anthony Storr (Ballantine: New York, 1988). An exploration of solitude and its role in the lives of creative, fulfilled individuals.

Learned Optimism, by Martin E. P. Seligman (Pocket Books: New York, 1990). An important book about cognitive therapy.

Mind, Mood and Medicine, by Paul H. Wender, M.D., and Donald F. Klein, M.D. (Meridian: New York, 1982). A seminal book on the use of medications in the treatment of psychiatric disorders.

SIGNS OF
DEPRESSION

*D*epression has associated with it a number of symptoms. These symptoms cannot be easily stopped or controlled. They are part of the expression of depression.

These symptoms have been specified in what is called the DSM-III-R (Diagnostic and Statistical Manual for Mental Disorders), a guidebook used by therapists and other mental health professionals. Symptoms used in assessing depression in adults are not necessarily accurate when assessing depression in children or adolescents. Symptoms for adults, children, and adolescents can be hidden in everyday behavior and, therefore, may be overlooked.

The most useful layperson's description of symptoms in adults can be found in Jack Engler and Daniel Goleman's excellent book, *The Consumer's Guide to Psychotherapy*.

A Description of Depression

Depression is often referred to as *affective disorder* and is divided into two basic categories: unipolar disorder and bipolar disorder.

Unipolar Disorder

When people talk about "depression," they are usually referring to unipolar disease. Engler and Goleman describe four main categories of major depression: mood, depressing thoughts, physical symptoms and complaints, changes in behavior. Specifically these symptoms include the following:

MOOD
- Sadness. A feeling of intense, perpetual sadness, despondence, hopelessness, and gloom.
- Loss of pleasure and interest. People with depression feel a profound loss of interest in life. They are indifferent to what used to give them pleasure.
- Boredom.
- Anxiety. A sense of tension or feelings of panic.
- Turmoil. Brooding, worrying, and irritability.

THOUGHTS
- Persistent thoughts of being worthless or of guilt. An obsession with all one's faults and failures and remorse about wrongs one has committed.
- A negative view of the world, yourself, and life. Nothing seems good or worthwhile.
- Hopelessness and helplessness. A person feels the depression will go on forever and that the future is bleak.
- Inability to concentrate or remember. Everyday tasks such as reading a newspaper or watching television are very hard.
- Confusion and indecision. Thoughts become jumbled or slowed down; decisions become increasingly difficult.
- Hallucinations and delusions. Seeing or hearing things that are not there or believing imagined events have happened.

- Thoughts of death and suicide. Thinking about killing yourself.

PHYSICAL SYMPTOMS AND COMPLAINTS
- Changes in appetite and weight. Either eating a great deal and gaining weight or losing appetite and losing weight.
- Disturbance in sleep. Difficulty in falling asleep or staying awake.
- Sluggishness. Everything is slowed down—walking, eating, thinking, reacting.
- Agitation. Fidgeting, pacing, wringing hands.
- Lethargy. A loss of vitality and stamina.
- Loss of sexual appetite. Both an absence of desire and a lack of enjoyment in sex.
- Bodily complaints. These include back and neck aches, muscle cramps, headaches, blurred vision. Gastrointestinal disturbances, including nausea, heartburn, indigestion, and abdominal pain are also common.

BEHAVIOR
- Loss of interest in usual roles, such as spouse, parent, student, or employee.
- Loss of interest in normal activities.
- Clinging and demanding in relationships.
- Escape, such as withdrawing into solitude, staying in bed all day, etc.
- Excess, such as eating too much, taking drugs, or heavy drinking.
- Restlessness. Constant fidgeting, chain-smoking, spending sprees.
- Suicidal gestures. Attempts on one's life.

Bipolar Disorder

Also known as manic depression, bipolar disorder is so called because the sufferer's moods and behavior swing between two opposite "poles"—mania and depression. Mild forms of mania are known as hypomania.

A manic episode can be considered under way if a person displays several of these symptoms for at least a week, to the point that they disrupt the person's life or intrude on others who are close to them.

Specific symptoms for periods of mania include the following:

- Extreme elation, an expansive mood that lasts for days or weeks at a time.
- Irritability and belligerence if thwarted or frustrated; elation can suddenly turn to hostility and anger.
- Grandiosity, an unrealistically inflated self-image.
- Poor judgment, such as buying sprees, sexual binges, foolish investments while acting on whim.
- Incessant activity and excitement in pursuit of an ever-changing set of goals.
- Pressured speech—talking a blue streak, often with utter disregard for what others say.
- Fluidity of thought and free association, jumping from one topic to another.
- Lack of need for sleep, staying up for days at a time or getting by on a few hours of sleep.
- Distractibility, so that attention is readily drawn by trivial things or irrelevancies.
- Intrusiveness and thoughtlessness, acting headstrong and demanding, pushing family and friends to the limits.

Periods of mania are followed by a "crash"—depression—the symptoms of which are listed above under "Unipolar Disorder."

Manic depression is often misdiagnosed and misunderstood. Extreme forms of manic depression can cause suicide, as well as violent and criminal behavior.

Depression in Children and Adolescents

Not only adults become depressed. Significant depression exists in about 5 percent of children and adolescents in the general population. Youngsters in hospitals and special education centers have higher rates of depression.

Depressed children and teenagers behave differently than depressed adults. According to the American Academy of Child and Adolescent Psychiatry, parents should be aware of the following signs of depression:

- Persistent sadness.
- No longer enjoys or looks forward to favorite activities.
- Increased activity or irritability.
- Frequent complaints of physical illness such as headaches and stomachaches.
- Frequent absences from school or poor performance in school.
- Persistent boredom, low energy, poor concentration.
- A major change in eating and/or sleeping patterns.

A depressed child who used to play often with friends may start spending a lot of time alone. Activities that were once fun may now bring little joy. Depressed children and adolescents may say they want to be dead or may talk about suicide. Or they may abuse alcohol or other drugs.

Many children and adolescents who cause trouble at home or at school may actually be depressed but their parents and teachers may not know it. Because the youngsters may not seem sad, parents and teachers may not realize that troublesome behavior is a sign of depression.

Early diagnosis and medical treatment are essential for depressed children. For help, parents can ask their physician to refer them to a child and adolescent psychiatrist who can diagnose and treat depression in children and teenagers. A child and adolescent psychiatrist is a physician with at least 5 years of additional training beyond medical school in child and adolescent psychiatry.

Psychologists and social workers counseling families, children, and adolescents should also have special training.

Don't forget, depression can be effectively treated, but untreated it can be life-threatening.

ACKNOWLEDGMENTS

*T*he making of this book involved a vast community of individuals. Some of the individuals were my therapists, some were my teachers, some my family, some told me their stories, some offered professional advice, some had me for dinner, some for the night, some for the month. Some argued with me, forcing me to hone my theories. Some hugged me. Some loved me. Some did the above and more. All were my healers. When I wrote the original version of the acknowledgments the list of their names was so long it filled nine pages. The list overwhelmed the text, the publisher told me—I would have to cut it.

Who should I include? How could I honor the individuals whose names I couldn't include? I decided on trust and hope. I hoped that each individual not specifically mentioned would trust my intent. And I hoped they would trust my gratitude and respect for their contributions.

The making of this book was a lengthy process also. The most demanding moments came at a time of great transition in my daughters' lives. I am grateful to them for enduring, for loving me over the years despite my worst self, and for continuing to challenge me with their intelligence, intuition, wisdom, and truth.

I am blessed with what I call "my support network": friends, healers, advisers, and guides who helped me recover and continue to encourage me to act on my dreams. Peter Cameron-Gilsey, my talented cousin, has with professional expertise as a psychotherapist, personal knowledge of our family histories, and unconditional love nurtured my mind and my spirit. Katharine B. Davis and Evelyn K. Frost have stood by me, provided me with homes, encouraged me to write, patiently listened to each new scheme, endured my idiosyncrasies and rages. Christopher Gates engineered my recovery for eight years. Rylin Malone changed the quality of my life and opened the door to my spiritual self.

My women's group—Julia M., Julia E., Grace, Margie, and Sarah—teach me about emotional safety and intimacy. Elizabeth Winthrop, single-handedly, is friend, editor, mentor, philosophy professor, and inspiration.

Howard Medwed and Harris Coles advocate for me with unconditional generosity, giving me faith that my vision of working from the heart is possible.

Jean Baker Miller, William Beardslee, and Sam Yanes believed in me before I believed in myself and agreed to support me in the founding of The Depression Initiative (TDI). Besides being executive board members of TDI, Jean, Bill, and Sam have been invaluable guides. Bill needs special mention for his unfaltering friendship and his compassionate work with intervention, prevention, and family treatment as essential in healing depression.

I am especially grateful to Shervert Frazier, a member of TDI's advisory board, for his wisdom and expertise, his personal and professional guidance, and his willingness to support my vision.

It took a long time to gain the confidence to write anything, let alone a book. Sally Jackson fueled that confidence
with her computers, office space, and editorial skills. Wendy
Mnookin and Laurie Robertson-Lorant, fellow poets and
mothers, wouldn't let me quit.

At the heart of my support network is a plethora of friends.
There are my friends in Massachusetts, Maine, and New York
who wine and dine me, hug, dance, argue, and walk with me,
answer my late-night phone calls, tease, edit, and care for my
children. My friends in Wyoming—a blessing with a life of its
own—keep me honest, healthy, compassionate, and on track.
In Utah my friends tuck me in, screen my calls, talk me
through philosophical hard spots, and take me fishing. For
more than 30 years, my Italian friends have welcomed me
home and reminded me of the importance of soul, laughter,
passion, and beauty.

Four years ago, bolstered by my support network, I released
the dream of a book on depression into the greater world. I
had no idea how it would land. Its existence, like my recovery, is the result of teamwork and talented professional
advice. I am grateful to Jill Kneerim and Sarah Flynn, who
worked hard to make my original concept a reality.

From the mistakes of those first efforts came Larry
Rothstein, my collaborator, who not only helped me form the
book but encouraged me through the hard spots with laughter and compassion.

Larry guided me to Kristine Dahl, my agent at International Creative Management. She has my gratitude for
believing in my dream and escorting it efficiently to Janet
Goldstein at HarperCollins. Janet understood immediately
what I was trying to communicate. She and Peternelle van
Arsdale, her assistant, gently nudged my dream into reality.
Thank you.

Irene Stiver and Alvin Poussaint, TDI advisory board members, have my sincere appreciation for helping to outline the contents of this book. I am also grateful to Ellen Poss and Warren Kantrowitz for their early support.

Evie Barkin, the president of the Manic Depressive and Depressive Association of Boston, has provided infinite wisdom. She made it possible for me to meet and talk with many of the members of MDDA and to share their stories and expertise. Without Evie and MDDA much of this book might not have evolved.

I am grateful to Paul Wender and Bennett Gurian for so readily sharing their research and time, to Miriam Gilpatric for making it financially possible to develop the proposal, and to Serita Winthrop for gracefully enduring my early doubts, indecisions, and transitions.

The editorial skills of Natalie Wigotsky and Nicholas Frost, practiced with such honesty and intelligence, kept me on course. Clarissa Smith, herbalist and nutritionist, generously contributed her knowledge.

Elizabeth Valentine interrupted a departure.

Sandra Wadsworth gave me a cherished gift when she vowed, "You are not alone." My vocation was inspired in a single moment by my dear friend, Thomas Frost. I grieve the loss of their persons, but they have not left me.

Silvio Onesti has guided my family. Sarah Conn and George Bowman have guided my soul.

And I am grateful for Richard, his graceful intelligence, his elegant integrity, his gentle patience.